PRACTICE MAKES PERFECT™

Basic German

PRACTICE MAKES PERFECT™

Basic German

Jolene Wochenske

New York Chicago San Francisco Lisbon London Madrid Mexico City
Milan New Delhi San Juan Seoul Singapore Sydney Toronto

Contents

Preface

Willkommen! Welcome to *Practice Makes Perfect: Basic German,* a workbook to assist you in your first year of learning the German language.

If you are new to the language—as a self-study learner or a middle or high school student at the beginning level—this handy workbook can supplement a first-year textbook. If you are at the end of a first-year course or beginning a second-year course, this workbook can serve as a review text. And *Practice Makes Perfect: Basic German* can also be used in conjunction with a face-to-face or online German course. Whatever your needs, you hold in your hands a helpful overview of basic grammar, key verbs, structures, and other grammatical elements.

As with any language learning activities, be sure to have a basic dictionary of the language at hand. *Practice Makes Perfect: Basic German* presents high-frequency vocabulary words throughout the book, but absorbing them all at once can be challenging.

While this workbook is not meant to be a primary teaching tool, its nine parts and 46 chapters build on each other, progressing from simple concepts to complex ones. This format will help you learn, review, and retain your knowledge of basic vocabulary and grammatical structures. Use the exercises included in every chapter to test your comprehension. Use the detailed table of contents to follow the progression—or jump around in the book to the sections that you need practice on. The Answer key at the back of the book covers all exercises.

Sprinkled throughout the book are some "Fun facts"—some in English and some in German. For the German ones, try to read them for fun and understand them on your own (but so that you may check how much and how well you have understood, they are translated in the back of the book).

This book would not exist without some very key people.

- Holly McGuire, my editor, who believed in me and made this writing process fun and stress-free. Open to all ideas and there for guidance and assurance, she has been my backbone and support system.
- My past and present German teachers and students, who have taught me so many things, especially how to make complicated German easier to learn and how to let loose and just have fun.
- A huge **Danke schön!!!** to the person whose daily support, and willingness to take care of both babies while I locked myself in the office for hours, made this book possible—my husband, Steve. I never thought I deserved such a partner and best friend, and I am so grateful I have you.
- To my two babies, A. and M. You are the reason I live and breathe, and this book is for you. **Möge das Lachen in Euren Herzen tanzen und vergeßt nie, wie schön Ihr seid und wie sehr ich Euch liebe! Ihr seid wahre Engel auf Erden!**

Grammar

Vocabulary

Fun facts

The alphabet and pronunciation

German pronunciation is straightforward. Every letter in every word is enunci-ated. There is, of course, the occasional exception to this rule of thumb. Some-times a word might be pronounced differently in the case of a word being adopted from a different language. This may also happen if the speaker is using a regional dialect. The German alphabet has the same 26 letters as the English alphabet, but it also has three additional vowels (ä, ö, ü) and one additional consonant (ß).

Das Alphabet (*The alphabet*)

A	ah	Sand (*sand*), acht (*eight*)	like the short *ah* sound in *tot*
		Paß (*passport*), klar (*clear*)	like the long *ah* sound in *tar*
B	bay	Burg (*castle*), bis (*until*)	
C	say	Computer (*computer*), circa (*approximately*)	the first c like *s* in sinus, the second like *k*
D	day	Dach (*roof*), dann (*then*)	
E	eh/ay	Endung (*ending*), essen (*to eat*)	like the short *e* sound in *met*
		Ehe (*marriage*), eben (*just*)	like the long *ay* sound in *May*
F	eff	Fluss (*river*), fremd (*foreign*)	
G	gay	Geld (*money*), geben (*to give*)	
H	hah	Hitze (*heat*), hoch (*high*)	
I	ih/ee	ich (*I*), bitte (*please*)	like the short *i* sound in *with*
		Iren (*Irish*), wir (*we*)	like the long *ee* sound in *mirror*
J	yut	Juli (*July*), jeder (*each*)	like the *y* sound in *you*
K	kah	Kuh (*cow*), klein (*little*)	
L	el	Lampe (*lamp*), laut (*loud*)	
M	em	Morgen (*morning*), mehr (*more*)	
N	en	Neffe (*nephew*), neben (*next to*)	
O	o/oh	Sonne (*sun*), sollen (*should*)	like the short *o* sound in *hot* (very short)
		Ort (*place*), so (*so*)	like the long *oh* sound in *so* (very long)
P	pay	Prinz (*prince*), pro (*for*)	
Q	coo	Quarz (*quartz*), queren (*to cross*)	
R	er	Rentner (*retiree*), roh (*raw*)	
S	es	Sohn (*son*), seit (*since*)	
T	tay	Tag (*day*), treu (*loyal*)	

U	oo	Wut (*anger*), uns (*us*)	like the short *oo* sound in *truth*
		Kuß (*kiss*), putzen (*to clean*)	like the long *oo* sound in *true*
V	fow	Vogel (*bird*), viel (*much*)	
W	vay	Wasser (*water*), wann (*when*)	
X	iks	X-Beine (*knock-knees*), x-beliebig (*any*)	
Y	ipsilohn	Yoga (*yoga*)	
Z	tset	Zoo (*zoo*), zusammen (*together*)	

Special letters

Umlaute

In certain German words, two dots (i.e., umlauts) are placed above the vowel to change the sound of the original vowel sound. This occurs only with the vowels **a**, **o**, and **u**. The sound incorporates a combination of the sound created by the vowel and the sound of the letter *e*.

Ä

To create this sound, start by saying *met* and holding the *e*, then round your lips.

eh/ay   Äpfel (*apples*), älter (*older*)
         Mädchen (*girl*), ähnlich (*similar*)

Ö

To create this sound, say *ay* while rounding your lips.

ay   Löffel (*spoon*), öffnen (*open*)
      Föhn (*foehn*), schön (*pretty*)

Ü

To create this sound, start by saying *me* and hold the *e*, then round your lips.

oo   für (*for*)
      Glück (*happiness*)

ß Eszett or scharfes S

In modern-day German, the **ß** is used in place of a double **s** only in certain situations. According to the spelling reform of 1996, the **ß** is written after long vowel sounds and after vowel combinations (diphthongs). Vowel and consonant combinations will be covered more extensively in the following chapter.

After a long vowel:

saß (*sat*), but no ß in Fass (*barrel*)
groß (*big*), but no ß in Ross (*steed*)
außen (*external*), but no ß in muss (*must*)

After a diphthong:

ei   heiß (*hot*)
ie   ließ (*allowed*)

<table>
<tr><td>

ÜBUNG
1·1

</td></tr>
</table>

Buchstabieren (*Spelling*). *Spell the following English words from the German cues.*

1. pay—oh—es—tay   _____

2. bay—ah—el—el   _____

3. er—oo—en   _____

4. vay—ah—tay—say—hah   _____

5. coo—oo—ee—ay—tay   _____

Spaßfakten (*Fun facts*)

Die Rechtschreibreform (*Spelling reform*)

Just as the spelling of English words has changed through the centuries, the German language has as well. But you might be surprised to know that some of the spelling standards changed as recently as 1996. Here are some highlights of more than 130 years of fuss!

In July 1880, the Kingdom of Prussia declared the work of Konrad Duden to represent the official spelling of the German language. In 1901, another convention, the Staatliche Orthographie-Konferenz, determined the official spelling of the German language.

In 1936, Switzerland broke with other German-speaking countries and eliminated the ß from its written language.

In November 1955, Duden once again became the authority for the spelling and punctuation of German.

In 1991, after East Germany and West Germany were officially reunified, any differences in spelling between the two republics were eliminated to create a uniform language.

In 1996, the most recent reform of the German language took place. Because this 1996 spelling reform included so many new rules, the majority of the country protested its implementation. Although schools were required to teach the new rules and publishers were required to edit all written material according to the new rules, newspapers and other institutions throughout the country refused to use the new rules and instead continued to use the old ones. In fact, many authors and editors called for a revocation of the reform.

Even so, in July 1998, the German supreme court upheld the decision to reform the language. Until 2005, both systems were accepted, but after that year all schools, government bodies, and public institutions were required to adhere to the reform of 1996—and they were held accountable for correct spelling. In February of 2006, upon much protest, a final revision of the language reform was put into effect.

There are too many rules in the 1996 reform to discuss here, but two of the most prominent new rules are the replacement of the **ß** by **ss** following short vowels and a rule governing the addition of consonants that now allows words with triple consonants (as in **Flussschifffahrt**, *riverboat trip*).

Vowel combinations (diphthongs) and consonant combinations

2

Diphthongs

Diphthongs are vowel combinations, and vowel combinations are just what they sound like—a combination of vowels. There are two forms of vowel combinations: the **Umlaut** (see Chapter 1) and diphthongs. Diphthongs are created by combining two of four of the vowels (**a, e, i, u**), and the sound is made by combining the separate sounds of each vowel. Be careful not to pronounce each letter, but rather the combination of the two sounds.

au	Pronounced like the *ow* in the English word *now*. It is found in German words like **Haus** (*house*), **Maus** (*mouse*), **laufen** (*to run*), and **kaufen** (*to buy*).
äu, eu	Both are pronounced like the *oy* in the English word *boy*. They are found in German words such as **Häuser** (*houses*) and **Europa** (*Europe*).
ai, ei	These diphthongs are pronounced identically. The sound they make is like the English word *eye*. They are found in German words like **Mai** (*May*), **Hai** (*shark*), **eins** (*one*), and **Bein** (*leg*).
ie	This final diphthong is pronounced like the *ee* in the English word *tree*. It can be found in words such as **Biene** (*bee*), **sie** (*she* or *they*), and **fließen** (*to flow*).

Consonant combinations

Sometimes the two written consonants are pronounced as one consonant, which may or may not be one of the two that are written; sometimes the presence of one of the two consonants in the combination alters the pronunciation of the two together in a way that is just not what an English speaker might expect. Here are some examples:

ch	Chaos, Chor	k	found at the beginning of a word
	Chance	sh	found at the beginning of a word, mostly from French
	China	h	found at the beginning of a word, very heavy *h* sound
	ich, mich	ch (*like cat hiss*)	before bright vowel sound like *i* or *e*
	ach, doch	ch (*guttural*)	before heavy vowel sound like *a* or *o*

ck	der Rock (*skirt*)	k	same as English *k* sound
dsch	der Dschungel	dj	used in words that come from English to replace *j*
kn	das Knie	k-n	unlike in English, the k is actually pronounced
pf	pfeifen (*to whistle*)	pf	completely close lips for the p and follow with an f
ph	das Alphabet	f	same as English *f* sound
qu	die Quelle (*source*)	kv	quickly say both letters together
sch	der Schuh	sh	found at the beginning of a word
sp	spät (*late*)	shp	although there is no h in the spelling, the s as an English *sh* before the p
st	stur (*stubborn*)	sht	although there is no h in the spelling, the s as an English *sh* before the t
th	Thema (*theme*)	t	here the h is actually silent
tsch	tschechisch	ch	this combination is used to replace the English *ch*

ÜBUNG

2·1

Buchstabieren (*Spelling*). *Spell the following German words with vowel combinations from the German cues.*

1. el—oy—ef—tay   _____

2. em—ow—es   _____

3. bay—eye—en   _____

4. oy—er—oh   _____

ÜBUNG

2·2

Buchstabieren (*Spelling*). *Spell the following German words with consonant combinations from the German cues.*

1. sht—oo—er   _____

2. er—oh—k   _____

3. kv—ay—el—el—ay   _____

Subject pronouns

ich	I	**wir**	we
du	you (*singular, familiar*)	**ihr**	you (*plural, familiar*)
er	he		
sie	she	**sie**	they
es	it	**Sie**	you (*sing. or pl., formal*)

Er and **sie** can also mean "it" when referring in English to words that would normally be genderless (inanimate objects).

Noun cases
Definite and
indefinite articles

WORTSCHATZ			
Frau	woman	**Mädchen**	girl
Haus	house	**Mann**	man
Junge	boy	**Mutter**	mother
Kind	child	**Vater**	father
Kinder	children		

Das Substantiv und der Kasus
(*The noun and noun cases*)

A noun is a person, place, thing, or idea. When reading German it is simple to find a noun in a phrase or sentence—nouns are always capitalized.

> Der Junge isst vom Teller mit   *The boy eats from the plate using*
> dem Löffel und der Gabel.   *the spoon and the fork.*

In this sentence, the nouns are **Junge** (*boy*), **Teller** (*plate*), **Löffel** (*spoon*), and **Gabel** (*fork*).

In German, every noun needs a case (in English, we have cases, but we sometimes don't realize it). Depending on which particular case a German noun is in, its article can and will change. There are four cases in German: nominative (**Nominativ**), accusative (**Akkusativ**), dative (**Dativ**), and genitive (**Genitiv**).

Nouns can play many different roles, as these sentences demonstrate.

> *The boy presents a ring.*
> *The boy presents the girl with a ring.* (= *The boy presents a ring to the girl.*)
> *The boy presents the girl with his mother's ring.* (= *The boy presents his mother's ring to the girl.*)
> Der Junge schenkt dem Mädchen den Ring seiner Mutter.

The nominative is the subject, or the actor, in the sentence. The accusative is the direct object. The indirect object is called the dative. Finally, the genitive case usually demonstrates possession. The only change to the noun itself occurs in the dative case if the noun is masculine, or in the genitive case if the noun is masculine or neuter. An **-s** or **-es** is added to its ending, as in the following:

> des Mann**es** (one syllable)   *the man's*
> des Mädchen**s** (two or more   *the girl's*
>   syllables)

Definite articles (the)

	MASCULINE	FEMININE	NEUTER	PLURAL
Nominative	der Vater	die Mutter	das Haus	die Kinder
Accusative	den Vater	die Mutter	das Haus	die Kinder
Dative	dem Vater	der Mutter	dem Haus	den Kindern
Genitive	des Vaters	der Mutter	des Hauses	der Kinder

Nominative: Die Mutter ist schön.
Accusative: Wir sehen die Mutter.
Dative: Ich gebe der Mutter die Blumen.
Genitive: Das sind die Blumen der Mutter.

The mother is lovely.
We see the mother.
I give the flowers to the mother.
Those are the mother's flowers.

ÜBUNG
3·1

Change each of the following words and their gender based on the hint given. Include the definite article.

1. die Frau—dative _____

2. der Mann—genitive _____

3. das Haus—accusative _____

4. der Mann—dative _____

5. die Frau—genitive _____

Indefinite articles (*a, an*)

	MASCULINE	FEMININE	NEUTER	PLURAL
Nominative	ein Vater	eine Mutter	ein Haus	(k)eine Kinder
Accusative	einen Vater	eine Mutter	ein Haus	(k)eine Kinder
Dative	einem Vater	einer Mutter	einem Haus	(k)einen Kindern
Genitive	eines Vaters	einer Mutter	eines Hauses	(k)einer Kinder

Change each of the following words and their gender based on the hint given. Use the indefinite article.

1. die Frau—dative   _____

2. der Mann—genitive   _____

3. das Haus—accusative   _____

4. der Mann—dative   _____

5. die Frau—genitive   _____

Nouns—gender and definite articles Things in nature

Das Genus (*Gender*)

In addition to being capitalized, all German nouns have what is called grammatical gender. There are three genders (masculine, feminine, and neuter) plus the plural. These genders are shown by an article. When speaking about a particular or specific item, the gender of nouns is shown by a definite article, or a form of *the* (**der**, **die**, or **das**).

MASCULINE	FEMININE	NEUTER
der Mann	die Frau	das Kind
der Löffel	die Gabel	das Messer

ÜBUNG
4·1

*Write the correct article (**der**, **die**, or **das**) for each noun.*

1. (feminine) _____ Frau

2. (masculine) _____ Teller

3. (neuter) _____ Haus

4. (neuter) _____ Papier

5. (plural) _____ Jungen

6. (feminine) _____ Katze

7. (neuter) _____ Mädchen

8. (feminine) _____ Stereoanlage

9. (feminine) _____ CD

10. (masculine) _____ Garten

Kategorisierung des Genus (*Gender categorization*)

Most genders are random, so the best method for learning the gender of nouns is to memorize the gender with the noun. But some patterns do exist, which makes learning them much easier.

Masculine

Males, or male jobs: **der Mann** (*man*), **der Junge** (*boy*), **der Arbeiter** (*worker*)

Weather: **der Regen** (*rain*), **der Wind** (*wind*), **der Sturm** (*storm*)

Times (day, month, etc.): **der Montag** (*Monday*), **der Abend** (*evening*), **der Winter** (*winter*)

Cardinal directions: **der Norden** (*north*), **der Süden** (*south*), **der Osten** (*east*), **der Westen** (*west*)

Nouns ending in -**ich**, -**ig**, -**ling**, -**ismus**: **der Teppich** (*rug*), **der Honig** (*honey*), **der Frühling** (*spring*), **der Journalismus** (*journalism*)

Feminine

Females, or female jobs: **die Frau** (*woman*), **die Mutter** (*mother*), **die Astronautin** (*astronaut*)

Flowers: **die Rose, die Lilie, die Narzisse** (but not **das Schleierkraut**, *baby's breath*)

Cardinal numbers: **die Eins, die Zehn**

Most nouns ending in -**e**, -**ie**, or -**ei**: **die Hose** (*pants*), **die Symphonie, die Partei** (but not **der Name**, *name*, or **das Ei**, *egg*)

Nouns with the suffixes -**heit**, -**keit**, -**ion**, -**schaft**, -**tät**, -**ung**: **die Mehrheit** (*majority*), **die Möglichkeit** (*possibility*), **die Religion, die Mannschaft** (*team*), **die Universität, die Zeitung** (*newspaper*)

Most nouns ending in -**ik**: **die Musik** (but not **der Pazifik**)

Neuter

Names of countries, states, etc.: **das Deutschland, das Europa**

Letters of the alphabet: **das A und das O**

Verbs as gerunds: **das Laufen** (*running*)

Foreign words: **das Sofa**

Most metals: **das Gold** (but not **der Stahl**, *steel*)

Nouns ending in -**chen** or -**lein**: **das Mädchen** (*girl*), **das Männlein** (*little man*)

Most nouns ending in -**ment**, -**tum**, or -**um**: **das Monument, das Eigentum** (*property*), **das Studium** (*studies*)

Most nouns beginning with **Ge-**: **das Geschirr** (*dishes*) (but not **die Geburt**, *birth*)

WORTSCHATZ

arbeitet für	works for	**kurz**	short
das ist	that is	**sehe/siehst/sieht/sehen/seht**	forms of *to see*
duftet schön	smells beautiful	**sehr**	very
ich lese	I read	**sie**	she

Lücken ausfüllen. (*Fill in the blanks.*) *Complete the following by filling in the blanks with the correct forms of the definite article in the nominative case.*

1. Das ist _____ Vater.

2. Sie ist _____ Mutter.

3. _____ Astronautin arbeitet für NASA.

4. _____ Studium ist an der Universität.

5. _____ Rose duftet schön.

6. _____ Februar ist kurz.

7. Ich lese _____ Zeitung.

8. _____ Land ist sehr schön.

WORTSCHATZ

Die Natur (*Things in nature*)

der Baum	tree	**das Gebüsch**	bush
der Berg	mountain	**der Schnee**	snow
die Blume	flower	**der Wald**	forest
das Feld	field	**die Wolke**	cloud
der Fluss	river		

Lücken ausfüllen. (*Fill in the blanks.*) *Fill in the blank with the correct item of nature in the accusative case.*

1. Ich sehe _____ (*the tree*).

2. Wir sehen _____ (*the field*).

3. Er sieht _____ (*the snow*).

4. Siehst du _____ (*the cloud*)?

5. Ihr seht _____ (*the flowers*).

Andere Artikelwörter (Other words that function as articles)

Certain words function similarly to the definite article, but their meaning is much more specific. They take the same endings when declined in the various cases.

this/these	dies- (close to speaker)
that/those	jen- (away from speaker)
all	all- (singular or plural)
each, every	jed- (always singular)
which	welch-
some	manch- (almost always plural)
such	solch-

	MASCULINE	FEMININE	NEUTER	PLURAL
Nominative	dieser	diese	dieses	diese
Accusative	diesen	diese	dieses	diese
Dative	diesem	dieser	diesem	diesen +n
Genitive	dieses +(e)s	dieser	dieses +(e)s	dieser

All of the demonstrative pronouns follow this exact pattern. As with other pronouns, any of these demonstrative pronouns can modify a noun or stand alone.

Welchen Apfel möchtest du?
Ich möchte diesen (Apfel).

Jener is used relatively rarely in German, and instead of it one can use **dieser** (*this/that, these/those*).

ÜBUNG
4·4

Lücken ausfüllen. (Fill in the blanks.) *Using the same sentence, fill in the blank with the correct form of **dies-**.*

1. Wir kennen den Mann. Wir kennen _____ Mann.

2. Siehst du das Wasser? Siehst du _____ Wasser?

3. Er singt das Lied. Er singt _____ Lied.

4. Ihr macht die Übung. Ihr macht _____ Übung.

5. Kaufen Sie das Haus? Kaufen Sie _____ Haus?

6. Sie möchte den Mantel. Sie möchte _____ Mantel.

Übersetzung (*Translation*)

1. I would like that car.

_____

2. For which girl is he buying the flowers?

_____

3. Such houses are expensive.

_____

4. Every book is good.

_____

5. All flowers are pretty.

_____

6. Some clouds are not white.

_____

Nouns—gender and indefinite articles School and office supplies

Der unbestimmte Artikel
(The indefinite article)

As explained in Chapter 4, each noun in German has a specific grammatical gender (masculine, feminine, or neutral). This gender is shown by an article. As we saw in the previous chapter, when speaking about a particular or specific item, the gender of nouns is shown by a definite article, or a form of *the* (**der**, **die**, or **das**).

Indefinite articles (*a, an, one, any*) are used when one is speaking about a nonspecific noun. These nonspecific nouns normally do not have an article in the plural form.

Ein Junge isst von einem Teller mit einem Löffel und einer Gabel.	*A boy eats from a plate with a spoon and a fork.*

Masculine nouns are preceded by the word **ein** (pronounced *eye-n*), feminine nouns by **eine** (pronounced *eye-nah*), and neuter nouns by **ein**.

WORTSCHATZ

Apfel	apple	**möchte**	would like
deutscher	German	**Physiker**	physicist (*male*)
klein	small	**süß**	sweet
Lehrerin	teacher (*female*)	**war**	was

ÜBUNG

5·1

Lücken ausfüllen. (Fill in the blanks.) *Complete the following by filling in the blanks with the correct forms of the indefinite article in the nominative case.*

1. Einstein war _____ deutscher Physiker.

2. Sie ist _____ Dame.

3. Das Mädchen möchte _____ Blume.

4. _____ Apfel ist süß.

5. _____ Kind ist klein.

Die Schul-/Büroartikel (School and office supplies)

die Aktentasche	briefcase	der Kuli	pen
der Bleistift	pencil	das Lineal	ruler
der Buntstift	colored pencil	der Ordner	binder
der Büroklammer	paper clip	das Papier	paper
die CD	compact disc	das Prospekt	folder
der Computer	computer	der Radiergummi	eraser
der Drucker	printer	der Rucksack	backpack
der Füller	fountain pen	die Schere	scissors
das Heft	notebook	der Schrank	cabinet
die Heftmaschine	stapler	der Spitzer	pencil sharpener
der Klebstoff	glue	die Tafel	chalkboard
die Kreide	chalk	der Taschenrechner	calculator

ÜBUNG
5·2

Was brauchst du dafür? (What do you need for that?) Remember to write the
words in the accusative, because they are the direct object. Use the indefinite article.

1. zum schreiben (to write) _____

2. zum tippen (to type) _____

3. zum musikhören (to listen to music) _____

4. zum radieren (to erase) _____

5. zum schneiden (to cut) _____

6. zum zeichnen (to draw) _____

7. zum buntmalen (to color) _____

8. zum heften (to staple) _____

·II·

Grammar

Vocabulary

Compound nouns

WORTSCHATZ			
Buch	book	**Schule**	school
hoch	highly	**Stadt**	city
Liebling	favorite	**Straße**	road, street
schlafen	sleep	**Zimmer**	room

Das zusammengesetzte Substantiv (*Compound nouns*)

A compound noun is a word that is composed of at least two nouns. The noun that is in the final position in the compound word is the word that determines the gender and the plural form for the entire word. Here are some examples of common compound nouns in German.

das Streichholzschächtelchen	Streich—holz—schächtelchen (*matchbox*)
die Hauptstadt	Haupt—stadt (*capital city*)
der Tannenbaum	Tannen—baum (*evergreen tree*)

In some cases, it is essential to add a letter or letters between the nouns. For example, sometimes one must add the letter **s** or the letters **es**.

der Lieblingsfilm	Liebling—(s)—film (*favorite film*)
das Bundesland	Bund—(es)—land (*federal state*)

In other cases one must add an **n** or an **en** before adding an additional noun to the first noun. **N** is usually added to words that end in **e**.

die Jungenschule	Junge(n)—schule (*boys' school*)
der Krankenwagen	Krank(en)—wagen (*ambulance*)

Sometimes compound nouns contain adjectives or other parts of speech.

der Rotkohl	Rot—kohl (*red cabbage*)
das Rentier	Renn(en)—tier (*reindeer*)

Hinweis (*Note*): Because of the spelling reform, it is possible for a German compound noun to have three of the same letter in a row. This happens when a noun that ends in a double letter is combined with another noun that begins with the same letter. Here are some examples:

> die Flussschifffahrt (*riverboat trip*)
> die Bestellliste (*order form*)
> die Programmmusik (*program music*)
> der Rollladen (*metal window shutter*)

Lücken ausfüllen. (*Fill in the blanks.*) *Fill in the blanks with the correct compound nouns. Choose the correct gender based on the cues given. If the item has an asterisk (*), then add an extra letter (-**e**, -**es**, -**n**, or -**en**).*

1. (das Auto, der Bus) _____ ist hier.

2. * s (der Liebling, das Buch) _____ ist Harry Potter.

3. (hoch, das Haus) _____ ist in New York.

4. (der Schlaf, das Zimmer) _____ ist groß.

5. * n (die Straße, die Lampe) _____ ist kaputt.

Noun plurals
In the house
Numbers

Die Pluralformen (*Plurals*)

Unlike in English, the German plural is complex. Only one thing is consistent in German: all plurals take on the article **die**.

There is no perfect way to memorize the plural form. As with articles, when a learner sees the word for the first time, it is best to learn the word with its gender and plural immediately.

You can, however, see a few patterns in the German plural:

Foreign words

Most words that originate in foreign languages or nouns that end in a vowel will take an **-s** ending in the plural.

> Auto—Autos
> Restaurant—Restaurants
> Zoo—Zoos
> Café—Cafés

Words ending in -e

Most words ending in **-e** are also feminine. These nouns take an **-n** ending in the plural.

> Katze—Katzen
> Blume—Blumen

Umlaut + -er

Some words that contain vowels in their stem will add an umlaut over a vowel and end in **-e** or **-er** in the plural.

> Ball—Bälle
> Maus—Mäuse
> Stuhl—Stühle
> Kind—Kinder
> Buch—Bücher

Monosyllabic words

If a word has one syllable, sometimes one can simply add an **e** in the plural, although there are many exceptions to this pattern.

Tisch—Tische
Tag—Tage
Schuh—Schuhe

Words ending in -el or -er

These words usually stay the same and do not change in the plural, unless there is an umlaut added to a vowel in the stem.

Mantel—Mäntel
Taschenrechner—Taschenrechner
Schüler—Schüler

Words ending in -in

Words ending in **-in** are often words describing to women or related to jobs a woman would have. Here one adds **-nen** to the end of the word in the plural.

Freundin—Freundinnen
Schülerin—Schülerinnen
Lehrerin—Lehrerinnen
Köchin—Köchinnen

Words ending in -chen

This form is called the diminutive form. Here there is usually no change from the original word in the plural, other than to possibly add an umlaut in the stem.

Mädchen—Mädchen
Haus—Häuschen

Words that cannot be put into a plural form

Just like in English with *water*, *sugar*, and *metal*, to name a few, certain nouns in German cannot be made into the plural. These are called mass nouns.

Obst	*fruit*
Papier	*paper*
Butter	*butter*

Im Haus (*In the house*)

der Dachboden (Dachböden)	attic	das Haus (Häuser)	house
der Keller	basement	die Küche (Küchen)	kitchen
das Badezimmer	bathroom	das Wohnzimmer	living room
das Schlafzimmer	bedroom	das Heimbüro (Heimbüros)	office
der Schrank (Schränke)	closet	die Veranda (Veranden)	porch
das Esszimmer	dining room	das Zimmer	room
die Tür (Türen)	door	die Dusche (Duschen)	shower
das Foyer (Foyers)	foyer	die Badewanne (Badewannen)	tub
die Garage (Garagen)	garage	das Fenster	window
der Gang (Gänge)	hall	der Garten (Gärten)	yard; garden

ÜBUNG
7·1

Übersetzung (*Translation*). *Write the German plural. Include the definite article.*

1. garages   _____

2. basements   _____

3. doors   _____

4. yards   _____

5. halls   _____

Die Zahlen (*Numbers*) 1–10

eins	one	sechs	six
zwei	two	sieben	seven
drei	three	acht	eight
vier	four	neun	nine
fünf	five	zehn	ten

ein paar	a couple	mehrere	several
einige	a few	viel	much/many (with adjective ending)
keine	no	es gibt	there are

Lücken ausfüllen. (*Fill in the blanks.*) *Fill in the blanks with the correct form of each plural noun.*

1. (das Zimmer) Im Haus sind fünf _____.

2. (das Fenster) Im Badezimmer gibt es zwei _____.

3. (die Lampe) Im Schlafzimmer gibt es drei _____.

4. (der Stuhl) Im Esszimmer gibt es acht _____.

5. (der Baum) Im Garten gibt es viele _____.

6. (die Blume) In der Küche gibt es keine _____.

7. (das Auto) In der Garage gibt es ein paar _____.

8. (das Haustier) Im Wohnzimmer gibt es mehrere _____.

Personal pronouns
Spielen (to *play*)

Personal pronouns

A pronoun is a word that replaces, or is substituted for, a noun.

NOMINATIVE	ACCUSATIVE	DATIVE	GENITIVE
ich (*I*)	mich (*me*)	mir (*to/for me*)	mein (*my*)
du (*you*)	dich (*you*)	dir (*to/for you*)	dein (*your* [*singular, informal*])
er (*he*)	ihn (*him*)	ihm (*to/for him*)	sein (*his*)
sie (*she*)	sie (*she*)	ihr (*to/for her*)	ihr (*her*)
es (*it*)	es (*it*)	ihm (*to/for it*)	sein (*its*)
wir (*we*)	uns (*us*)	uns (*to/for us*)	unser (*our*)
ihr (*you*)	euch (*you*)	euch (*to/for you*)	euer (*your* [*plural, informal*])
sie (*they*)	sie (*them*)	ihnen (*to/for them*)	ihr (*their*)
Sie (*you*)	Sie (*you*)	Ihnen (*to/for you*)	Ihr (*your* [*formal*])

Er and **sie** can also mean "it," because gender isn't necessarily physical, but grammatical.

Conjugation of spielen

spielen (*to play*)	
ich spiel**e**	wir spiel**en**
du spiel**st**	ihr spiel**t**
er spiel**t**	sie spiel**en**
sie spiel**t**	Sie spiel**en**
es spiel**t**	

Konjugierung (*Conjugation*). *Conjugate the following verbs, using the conjugation of* **spielen** *as a model.*

ich	du	er/sie/es	wir	ihr	sie/Sie

1. spielen (*to play*)

_____ _____ _____ _____ _____ _____

2. sagen (*to say*)

_____ _____ _____ _____ _____ _____

3. machen (*to make/do*)

_____ _____ _____ _____ _____ _____

4. gehen (*to go*)

_____ _____ _____ _____ _____ _____

5. schauen (*to watch*)

_____ _____ _____ _____ _____ _____

6. hören (*to hear*)

_____ _____ _____ _____ _____ _____

7. kochen (*to cook*)

_____ _____ _____ _____ _____ _____

8. springen (*to jump*)

_____ _____ _____ _____ _____ _____

9. lachen (*to laugh*)

_____ _____ _____ _____ _____ _____

10. lernen (*to study*)

_____ _____ _____ _____ _____ _____

Übersetzung (*Translation*)

1. I jump. _____

2. You (sing. informal) say. _____

3. She says. _____

4. They study. _____

5. You (pl. informal) study. _____

6. You (formal) dance. _____

7. We dance. _____

8. He cooks. _____

9. We cook. _____

10. It dances. _____

11. He hears. _____

12. You (sing. informal) hear. _____

13. They watch. _____

14. I play. _____

15. It plays. _____

16. We go. _____

Stimmt das oder stimmt es nicht? (*True or false?*) *Mark the following statements true (**S**) or false (**SN**).*

1. _____ Ich lerne Spanisch.

2. _____ Wir tanzen im Schwimmbad.

3. _____ Er kocht Eis.

4. _____ Sie hören Musik.

Case and pronoun review Schenken (to give as a present)

·9·

Case and pronoun review

Let's take a moment to review what we've learned about case and pronouns.

Der Kasus (*Case*)

Nominative means the subject (for example, *we*).
Accusative means the direct object or object of an accusative preposition (*us*).
Dative means the indirect object or the object of a dative preposition (*to us*).
Genitive shows possession or ownership and can be demonstrated (in English) by either *'s* or the preposition *of* (*our*).

Der Nominativ (*Subject pronouns*)

ich	*I*	wir	*we*
du	*you (sing., informal)*	ihr	*you (pl., informal)*
er	*he*	sie	*they (pl.)*
sie	*she*	Sie	*you (sing. or pl., formal)*
es	*it*		

Der Akkusativ (*Direct object pronouns*)

mich	*me*	uns	*us*
dich	*you (sing., informal)*	euch	*you (pl., informal)*
ihn	*him*	sie	*them*
sie	*her*	Sie	*you (formal)*
es	*it*		

Die Frau mag **den** Hund.
Die Frau mag **ihn**.

Wir sehen **die** Schule.
Wir sehen **sie**.

Ich kaufe **das** Haus.
Ich kaufe **es**.

Meine Familie isst **die** Bonbons.
Meine Familie isst **sie**.

It is important to note that "it" assumes the gender of the noun it is replacing. So if a noun is masculine (**Hund**), it will actually be **er**, **ihn**, or **ihm**, depending on the case . . . not **es**! The same is true for feminine nouns (**sie**, **sie**, or **ihr**) and plural nouns (**sie**, **sie**, or **ihnen**).

The greeting typically heard in the southern part of Germany is also a perfect example of the accusative.

Grüß dich!   (*Hello!* or *I greet you!*)
Grüßt euch!   (*Hello!* or *I greet you all!*)

Übersetzung (*Translation*). *Translate the following sentences (or pairs of sentences).*

1. I buy the book. _____

   I buy it. _____

2. He has a chair. _____

   He has it. _____

3. She buys the coat. _____

   She buys it. _____

4. We see the cat (**Katze**). _____

   We see it. _____

5. They hear the girls. _____

   They hear them. _____

6. We see you all (informal). _____

7. The boy likes you (sing., informal). _____

Übersetzung (*Translation*). *Translate the following pairs of sentences.*

1. I have the books. _____

   I have them. _____

2. We have the cars. _____

   We have them. _____

3. They see the flowers. _____

   They see them. _____

Der Dativ (*Indirect object pronouns*)

mir	*to/for me*	uns	*to/for us*
dir	*to/for you (sing., informal)*	euch	*to/for you (pl., informal)*
ihm	*to/for him*	ihnen	*to/for them*
ihr	*to/for her*	Ihnen	*to/for you (formal)*
ihm	*to/for it*		

Unlike in the accusative, where the feminine, neuter, and plural pronouns are identical to the nominative, in the dative all pronouns change.

Der Kuli gehört **dem** Lehrer.
Er gehört **ihm**.

Der Mann dankt **der** Frau.
Der Mann dankt **ihr**.

Ich gratuliere **dem** Mädchen.
Ich gratuliere **ihm**.

Die Schüler hören **den** Lehrern zu.
Die Schüler hören **ihnen** zu.

Certain prepositions also require the dative. They will be covered further in Chapters 38 and 40.

Alle gehen an die Uni ausser **euch**.   *Everyone is going to the university except for you.*
Der Hund schläft immer bei **mir**.   *The dog always sleeps next to me.*

ÜBUNG
9·3

For each statement, write the direct object and indirect object (in English) in the blanks provided in the respective columns. Note that some of the objects are expressed as nouns, and some are expressed as pronouns.

	DIRECT OBJECT	INDIRECT OBJECT
1. We give the toy to him.	_____	_____
2. She gives the student the pen.	_____	_____
3. I send you a letter.	_____	_____
4. They tell us a story.	_____	_____
5. He writes a card for me.	_____	_____
6. You tell the girl a lie.	_____	_____
7. You read your child a book.	_____	_____
8. She sends me a present.	_____	_____

Conjugation of **schenken**

Schenken *(To give as a present)*

ich schenke	wir schenken
du schenkst	ihr schenkt
er schenkt	sie schenken
sie schenkt	Sie schenken
es schenkt	

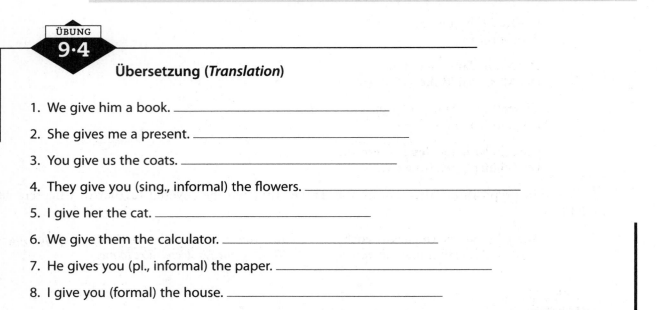

ÜBUNG
9·4

Übersetzung (*Translation*)

1. We give him a book. _____

2. She gives me a present. _____

3. You give us the coats. _____

4. They give you (sing., informal) the flowers. _____

5. I give her the cat. _____

6. We give them the calculator. _____

7. He gives you (pl., informal) the paper. _____

8. I give you (formal) the house. _____

Der Genitiv (*Pronouns of possession*)

Unlike pronouns in the other cases, pronouns in the genitive most often cannot stand alone. They are always followed by a noun in a noun phrase. These will be covered separately, in Chapter 10, because they are declined as possessive pronouns.

Possessive pronouns Family

Das Possessivpronomen
(*The possessive pronoun*)

Possessive pronouns are words that can, but do not have to, modify a noun, and they tell to whom the noun belongs. These pronouns function just like the indefinite articles, or **ein**-words. Their endings must reflect the case of the noun they modify.

Das Possessivpronomen

mein	*my*	unser	*our*
dein	*your* (*sing., informal*)	euer	*your* (*pl., informal*)
sein	*his*	ihr	*their*
ihr	*her*	Ihr	*your* (*formal*)
sein	*its*		

Hinweis (*Note*): If you add an -**e**, -**es**, or -**er** to **euer**, it can change to **eure/eures/eurer**.

WORTSCHATZ

Die Familie (*Family*)

der Großvater	grandfather	**die Großmutter**	grandmother
der Vater	father	**die Mutter**	mother
der Bruder	brother	**die Schwester**	sister
der Onkel	uncle	**die Tante**	aunt
der Cousin	male cousin	**die Kusine**	female cousin
die Geschwister (pl.)	siblings	**die Eltern** (pl.)	parents
die Großeltern (pl.)	grandparents	**Halb-**	half
Stief-	step	**das Haustier**	pet
der Hund	dog	**die Katze**	cat
der Fisch	fish		

Übersetzung (*Translation*)

1. That is my father. _____

   That is my mother. _____

   Those are my parents. _____

2. That is her sister. _____

   That is her brother. _____

   Those are her siblings. _____

3. That is your (sing., informal) pet. _____

   That is your (sing., informal) cat. _____

4. Those are our grandparents. _____

   That is our grandmother. _____

   That is our grandfather. _____

Übersetzung (*Translation*)

1. our father _____

2. their grandmother _____

3. your (sing., informal) siblings _____

4. my half sister _____

5. his mother _____

6. your (formal) grandfather _____

7. your (pl., informal) stepbrother _____

8. her male cousin _____

Wen kennst du? (*Whom do you know?*) *Write the correct form of the possessive pronoun in the accusative case.*

1. Kennst du _____? (my father)

2. Kennst du _____? (his sister)

3. Kennst du _____? (our grandfather)

4. Kennst du _____? (their parents)

5. Kennst du _____? (her uncle)

Das Possessivpronomen als Substantiv (*The possessive pronoun as a noun*)

When the possessive pronoun stands alone, it functions as a noun. When that happens, it is not modifying any noun. For example, if someone asks the general question *Is this your book?* in English, a person could answer *Yes, it's mine.* The same holds true in German.

Ist das dein Buch?	*Is this your book?*
Ja, es ist meins.	*Yes, it's mine.*

The ending of the possessive still needs to reflect the gender of the noun to which it refers, as you can see above. The gender of **das Buch** is neuter, therefore the ending is **-s.**

Masculine	meiner
Feminine	meine
Neuter	meins
Plural	meine

ÜBUNG
10·4

Write the correct response to the following questions using the cues.

1. Ist das sein Haus? Nein, das ist _____. (hers)

2. Ist das dein Rucksack? Nein, das ist _____. (yours, sing. informal)

3. Ist das mein Kuli? Nein, das ist _____. (mine)

4. Ist das ihre Schwester? Nein, das ist _____. (his)

5. Ist das unser Essen? Nein, das ist _____. (theirs)

6. Ist das mein Auto? Nein, das ist _____. (yours, pl. informal)

ÜBUNG
10·5

Wem schenkst du das? (*To whom are you giving that?*) *Write the correct form of the possessive pronoun in the dative case.*

1. Wir schenken _____ Eltern das Auto. (our)

2. Ich schenke _____ Freundin einen Ring. (my)

3. Sie schenkt _____ Mann eine Reise nach Deutschland. (her)

4. Schenkt ihr _____ Vater eine Uhr? (your, pl. informal)

5. Er schenkt _____ Frau Rosen. (his)

Genitive declension

Masculine	(mein)es, (*monosyllabic noun*)es, or (*multisyllabic noun*)s
Femine	(mein)er
Neuter	(mein)es, (*monosyllabic noun*)es, or (*multisyllabic noun*)s
Plural	(mein)er

ÜBUNG
10·6

Und wem gehört das jetzt? (*To whom does it now belong?*) *Write the correct form of the possessive pronoun in the genitive case.*

1. Das ist das Auto _____ Eltern. (their)

2. Das ist der Ring _____ Frau. (my)

3. Das ist das Haus _____ Großeltern. (your, pl. informal)

4. Das ist die Uhr _____ Vaters. (their)

5. Das ist der Käfig (*cage*) _____ Haustiers. (his)

·III·

Grammar

Vocabulary

Reflexive pronouns Body parts

Das Reflexivpronomen (The reflexive pronoun)

Reflexive pronouns are used when the verb is done by the subject, and the subject is also the object. These are activities that one does to oneself (e.g., shaving, combing hair, showering, etc.).

SUBJECT PRONOUN	ACCUSATIVE REFLEXIVE PRONOUN	DATIVE REFLEXIVE PRONOUN
ich	mich	mir
du	dich	dir
er	sich	sich
sie	sich	sich
es	sich	sich
wir	uns	uns
ihr	euch	euch
sie	sich	sich
Sie	sich	sich

In a sentence, the reflexive pronoun is almost always in the third position, or directly following the verb.

Ich interessiere mich für Musik.	*I am interested in music.*
Er tut sich den Kopf weh.	*He hurts his head.*
Wir erholen uns.	*We are recuperating.*

Das Reflexivpronomen im Akkusativ (The accusative reflexive pronoun)

There are two kinds of reflexive pronoun. The easier of the two is the accusative reflexive pronoun. They are used in sentences consisting of only the subject, the reflexive verb, and the accusative object. Some of the most commonly used accusative reflexive verbs are:

sich beeilen	*to hurry*
sich entscheiden	*to decide*
sich erholen	*to recuperate*
sich erkälten	*to catch a cold*
sich freuen	*to be happy*

Some accusative reflexive verbs also take an additional accusative object that is preceded by an accusative preposition.

sich erinnern an etwas	*to remember something*
sich freuen auf etwas	*to look forward to something*
sich gewöhnen an etwas	*to get used to something*
sich interessieren für etwas	*to be interested in something*

ÜBUNG
11·1

Übersetzung (*Translation*)

1. I'm hurrying. _____

2. We're happy. _____

3. They are recuperating. _____

4. You catch a cold. _____

5. He gets used to school. _____

6. She is excited about the party. _____

7. I remember the house. _____

Das Reflexivpronomen im Dativ (*The dative reflexive pronoun*)

The other kind of reflexive pronoun is the dative reflexive pronoun. When you use this case, you must also have an accusative object that is acted upon by the verb. Verbs used with this kind of pronoun typically refer to daily routines associated with the morning; there are substantially fewer reflexive verbs in the dative than in the accusative. Some of the most commonly used dative reflexive verbs are:

sich (etwas) putzen	*to clean, brush (teeth)*
sich (etwas) rasieren	*to shave (a body part)*
sich (etwas) verletzen	*to injure (a body part)*
sich (etwas) vorstellen	*to imagine (something)*
sich (etwas) waschen	*to wash (a body part)*
sich (etwas) weh tun	*to hurt (a body part)*

WORTSCHATZ

Die Körperteile (*Body parts*)

ankle	**der Fußknöchel, die Fußknöchel**	leg	**das Bein, die Beine**
arm	**der Arm, die Arme**	lip	**die Lippe, die Lippen**
back	**der Rücken**	mouth	**der Mund**
chin	**das Kinn**	muscle	**der Muskel, die Muskeln**
ear	**das Ohr, die Ohren**	neck	**der Hals** (throat), **der Nacken**
eye	**das Auge, die Augen**	nose	**die Nase**
face	**das Gesicht**	shoulder	**die Schulter, die Schultern**

finger	**der Finger, die Finger**	stomach	**der Bauch**
foot	**der Fuß, die Füße**	thumb	**der Daumen, die Daumen**
hair	**das Haar, die Haare**	toe	**der Zeh, die Zehen**
hand	**die Hand, die Hände**	tooth	**der Zahn, die Zähne**
head	**der Kopf**	wrist	**das Handgelenk, die Handgelenke**
knee	**das Knie, die Knie**		

ÜBUNG
11·2

Lücken ausfüllen. (*Fill in the blanks.*) *Fill in each blank with the correct form of the reflexive pronoun.*

1. Hans rasiert _____ .

2. Jana rasiert _____ die Beine.

3. Wir putzen _____ die Zähne.

4. Ich putze _____ die Zähne.

5. Sie waschen _____ die Hände.

6. Du tust _____ das Knie weh.

7. Ihr verletzt _____ die Muskeln.

8. Ich stelle _____ mein Haus vor.

ÜBUNG
11·3

Sätze schreiben. *Using the cues given, write a complete sentence. Be sure to observe if the reflexive pronoun is accusative or dative.*

1. Max / sich erholen / jedes Wochenende

_____

2. Jana / sich interessieren / für Eishockey

_____

3. wir / sich rasieren / jeden Morgen

_____

4. ihr / sich freuen / auf die Party

_____

5. ich / sich putzen / die Zähne

_____

Demonstrative pronouns ◆12◆

The demonstrative pronoun is simply a pronoun that functions like the definite article and noun together and refers to items that are defined and specific. Demonstrative pronouns replace nouns, and they also receive more stress than standard definite articles.

Das Demonstrativpronomen
(The demonstrative pronoun)

der *or* dieser (close to speaker)	*this*
jener (away from speaker)	*that*
jeder	*each, every*
welcher	*which*
mancher	*some*
solcher	*such*

Hinweis (*Note*): **Der** is declined almost exactly like the definite article, but with one exception. The dative plural is **denen**, not **den**. To add emphasis and to differentiate between two items, you will often add **da/dort** (*that one there*) or **hier** (*this one here*) to the **der** pronoun.

	MASCULINE	FEMININE	NEUTER	PLURAL
Nominative	der	die	das	die
Accusative	den	die	das	die
Dative	dem	der	dem	denen

Sie möchte die dort.   *She would like that one there.*

ÜBUNG
12·1

*Short answer: answer the following questions using the correct form of the pronoun **der** and including the particle **da**.*

1. Welches Buch möchtest du? _____

2. Welche Schüler siehst du? _____

3. Welcher Hund bellt? _____

49

4. Welches Kleid ziehst du an? _____

5. Welchen Mann heiratet sie? _____

6. Welches Auto fahren wir? _____

7. Welchen Personen dankt er? _____

Dieser

Here is the root pattern for the pronoun **dieser**.

	MASCULINE	FEMININE	NEUTER	PLURAL
Nominative	dieser	diese	dieses	diese
Accusative	diesen	diese	dieses	diese
Dative	diesem	dieser	diesem	diesen +n
Genitive	dieses +(e)s	dieser	dieses +(e)s	dieser

All of the rest of the demonstrative pronouns follow this exact pattern. As with other pronouns, any of these demonstrative pronouns can modify a noun or stand alone.

> Welchen Apfel möchtest du?
> Ich möchte diesen (Apfel).

Jener is used relatively rarely in German, and instead of it one can use **dieser** (*this/that, these/those*).

ÜBUNG
12·2

Lücken ausfüllen. (Fill in the blanks.) *Fill in each blank with the correct form of* **dieser**.

1. Ich nehme jenen Mantel, nicht _____ .

2. Sie möchte das Auto da, nicht _____ .

3. Wir kaufen ein Haus in der Stadt, nicht _____ .

4. Er will schöne Blumen, nicht _____ .

5. Der Lehrer meint die Tafel da drüben, nicht _____ .

Indefinite pronouns

In German the indefinite pronoun is used to name a person, a thing, or a group of persons or things in nonspecific terms. This pronoun can also be used to indicate an approximate quantity (but not a definite one). Take this example in English:

> *One shouldn't park here.*

In this sentence, *one* refers to any person, no matter who he or she is.

> *Several children were playing by the river.*

Here, we know that there were not many children, but we are unsure of exactly how many were playing there. These pronouns function the same in German as in English.

Das Indefinitpronomen (*The indefinite pronoun*)

Pronouns describing people

man	*one, people in general*
jeder	*each*
jedermann	*each person—when referring to a female, one uses* jede
jemand	*someone, anyone—*irgendjemand *is more indefinite than* jemand
niemand	*no one*

The pronouns listed above refer to any person, no matter the gender, but their grammatical gender is masculine (except for **jede**, also mentioned in the list above). **Man** is usually used in the passive voice and almost always functions as the subject; when referring to a person in general as the object of the verb, a form of **einer** is used instead of **man**. It cannot be replaced by **er**, as this pronoun has its own distinct meaning.

These pronouns also need to be declined according to the case.

Nominative	jeder	jedermann	jemand	niemand
Accusative	jeden	jedermann	jemand(en)	niemand(en)
Dative	jedem	jedermann	jemand(em)	niemand(em)
Genitive	—	jedermanns	jemands	niemands

Only **man** cannot be declined; instead, one can use a form of **einer**.

Pronouns describing things

alles	*everything*
etwas	*something*
nichts	*nothing*
viel	*much*
wenig	*little*

Pronouns describing the plural

alle	*all, everyone*	manche	*some*
andere	*others*	mehrere	*several*
ein paar	*a few*	viele	*many*
einige	*a few*	wenige	*few*
keine	*none*		

ÜBUNG

13·1

Lücken ausfüllen. (*Fill in the blanks.*) *Place the correct form of each word given into the blanks.*

(JEDER)

1. _____ muss in die Schule gehen.

2. Wir machen mit _____ ein Spiel.

3. Kennst du _____ hier?

(NIEMAND)

4. Ich kenne _____ hier.

5. _____ war da.

6. Sie spielt mit _____ .

(MAN)

7. _____ darf hier nicht rauchen.

8. Wir sehen _____, den wir kennen.

9. Sie sprechen mit _____ nicht.

Lücken ausfüllen. (*Fill in the blanks*.) *Complete these sentences by filling in each blank with the correct form of the word given.*

1. (nothing) Er kann _____ .

2. (someone) _____ kommt.

3. (everyone) _____ waren da.

4. (a few) Wir sehen _____ da drüben.

5. (several) _____ haben sich angemeldet.

6. (some) Triffst du dich mit _____?

7. (something) Ich kaufe heute _____ .

Interrogative pronouns: who? what? which? how many/much?

The interrogative pronoun begins an interrogative question or statement. In other words, it introduces a question or statement that seeks information and/or an answer. It can refer either to a person (*Who?*) or to an inanimate concept (*What? When? Where? Why?* etc.).

Das Interrogativpronomen
(*The interrogative pronoun*)
Wer? and was?

Wer (*who*) denotes any person regardless of gender but occurs only in the masculine. It follows the same declension pattern as the definite article **der**. If a preposition is placed before **wer**, then it takes on the case that is ruled by that preposition (see Chapters 37–40).

Nominative	wer?	*who?*
Accusative	wen?	*who(m)?*
Dative	wem?	*(to/for) who(m)?*
Genitive	wessen?	*whose?*

Was (*what*) plays the same roles in the sentence or question but refers only to inanimate objects, not people.

Nominative	was?	*what?*
Accusative	was?	*what?*
Dative	was?	*what?*
Genitive	(wegen) was?	*(on account of) what?*

Hinweis (*Note*): Sometimes there is an exception! When referring to a group of people (for example, a music group), you can use **was**.

Was ist „Münchener Freiheit"?	*What is "Münchener Freiheit"?*

Lücken ausfüllen. (*Fill in the blanks.*) *For each blank provided fill in the correct form of* **wer** *(***wer, wen, wem, wessen***).*

1. _____ seht ihr am Wochenende?

2. An _____ (acc.) schreibst du den Brief?

3. Mit _____ (dat.) fährst du nach Hause?

4. _____ hat keinen Kuli?

5. _____ ist nicht in der Klasse?

6. _____ Auto steht in der Garage?

7. Für _____ sind die schönen Blumen?

8. _____ Kinder gehen nicht in die Schule?

Lücken ausfüllen. (*Fill in the blanks.*) *Fill in each blank with the correct form of either* **wer** *or* **was**.

1. _____ schenkst du deiner Mutter zum Geburtstag?

2. _____ kommt heute nicht zur Party?

3. _____ ist heute nicht in der Klasse?

4. _____ kann ich machen?

5. _____ ist sein Vater?

6. _____ haben wir für Hausaufgaben?

Welcher?

Welcher (*which*) functions much like **wer** except that it modifies a noun and cannot stand alone. It can refer to a person or an object, and its ending changes depending on the gender, number, and case of the noun it modifies.

	MASCULINE	FEMININE	NEUTER	PLURAL
Nominative	welcher	welche	welches	welche
Accusative	welchen	welche	welches	welche
Dative	welchem	welcher	welchem	welchen +n
Genitive	welches	welcher	welches	welcher

ÜBUNG 14·3

Fragestellung (*Asking a question*). *For each answer, write an appropriate question using the correct form of* **welch-**.

1. _____ Das ist mein Haus.

2. _____ Der Schüler ist Hans.

3. _____ Wir haben den Lehrer Herrn Schmitt.

4. _____ Rockmusik gefällt mir.

5. _____ An die Universität Mainz gehe ich.

Wie viele? (*How much/many?*)

This interrogative pronoun measures either mass or quantity. It has only two forms: the singular and the plural (it does not differentiate in the singular based on gender). In the singular it does, however, act like the masculine, although it refers to feminine or neuter nouns as well.

SINGULAR	PLURAL
wie viel	wie viele

It is not customary to use **wie viel** in the genitive case.

ÜBUNG 14·4

Lücken ausfüllen. (*Fill in the blanks.*) *Choose the correct form of* **wie viel** *to place in each blank.*

1. _____ ist das?

2. _____ sind im Auto?

3. In _____ (dat.) gibt es einen Fluss? (Ländern)

4. _____ essen wir?

5. Mit _____ fahren wir nach New York? (Autos)

6. _____ siehst du am Wochenende? (Leute)

7. _____ spielen Fußball? (Schüler)

8. _____ esst ihr? (Kekse)

Adjectives

15

An adjective is a descriptive word used to modify a noun. Usually it will describe a characteristic, but the adjective can also simply mean *the*. We have already seen a few forms of this adjective—the definite and indefinite articles. Adjectives that describe a characteristic of the noun such as appearance, size, and stature can be used alone or within a noun phrase. Here are some lists that show just a few of all the possible adjectives.

Das Adjektiv (*Adjectives*)

WORTSCHATZ

Das Aussehen (*Appearance*)

dick	heavy	**alt**	old	**lockig**	curly
dünn	skinny	**jung**	young	**glatt**	straight
groß	tall, large	**neu**	new		
klein	short, small	**kurz**	short		
häßlich	ugly	**lang**	long		
schön	beautiful	**sauber**	clean		
hübsch	pretty	**schmutzig**	dirty		

Die Farbe (*Color*)

rot	red	**blond**	blond(e)
orange	orange	**dunkel**	dark
gelb	yellow	**hell**	light
grün	green	**braun**	brown
blau	blue	**schwarz**	black
lila	purple	**grau**	gray
weiß	white		

Hinweis (*Note*): When saying that something is a particular color, certain colors (**orange**, **lila**, **rosa**, etc.) must add the suffix -**farben**.

Der Geschmack (*Taste*)

süß	sweet	**bitter**	bitter
sauer	sour	**gut**	good
salzig	salty	**schlecht**	bad
scharf	spicy		

Die Persönlichkeit (Personality)

nett	nice	interessant	interesting
böse	evil, bad	langweilig	boring
faul	lazy	stark	strong
fleißig	industrious	schwach	weak
glücklich	happy	leise	quiet
traurig	sad	laut	loud
intelligent	intelligent		
dumm	dumb		
klug	clever		

Die Nationalität (Nationality)

amerikanisch	American	deutsch	German
französisch	French	spanisch	Spanish
türkisch	Turkish	britisch	British

Sonstiges (Miscellaneous)

bequem	comfortable	leicht	easy
eng	tight	schwer	difficult
weit	broad, far	langsam	slow
nah	near	schnell	fast
heiß	hot	billig	cheap
kalt	cold	teuer	expensive
warm	warm	hoch	high
halb	half	tief	low
reich	rich	arm	poor
gesund	healthy	krank	sick, ill
ganz	entire		

Conjugation of *sein*

sein *(to be)*	
ich bin	wir sind
du bist	ihr seid
er ist	sie sind
sie ist	Sie sind
es ist	

Das Adjektiv ohne Endung (*Adjectives without endings*)

When you use the verbs **sein** (*to be*), **werden** (*to become*), or **bleiben** (*to remain*), the adjective will follow the verb at the end of the sentence. It will not change in its base form, and it describes the noun. This is the simplest form because nothing happens to the adjective.

Übersetzung (*Translation*)

1. I am tall. _____

2. He is skinny. _____

3. We are rich. _____

4. They are nice. _____

5. Are you (*pl.*) happy? _____

6. You (*formal*) are pretty. _____

7. The car is fast. _____

8. The table is ugly. _____

9. My uncle is heavy. _____

10. Superman is not evil. _____

Das Adjektiv mit Endung (*Adjectives with endings*)

When you place the adjective in front of the noun, it then must be changed to match the noun's gender, role, and number. This can happen with any verb, and the ending depends on if there is an article or not. Because this will be explained more extensively in Chapter 16, here we will stick to adjectives describing nouns without an article.

	MASCULINE	FEMININE	NEUTER	PLURAL
Nominative	-er	-e	-es	-e
Accusative	-en	-e	-es	-e
Dative	-em	-er	-em	-en
Genitive	-en	-er	-en	-er

Eine Liste machen. *Create a list, using the cues given, of what is necessary in life.*

1. Freunde haben (gut) _____

2. Einkunft haben (sicher) _____

3. in Urlaub fahren (schön) _____

4. mit Kindern spielen (eigen) _____

5. Speisen essen (toll) _____

6. Geld verdienen (gut) _____

7. trotz Probleme glücklich sein (klein) _____

Lücken ausfüllen. (*Fill in the blanks*.) *Fill in the blanks with the correct form of each adjective given.*

1. Das ist _____ Kaffee (gut).

2. Wir haben _____ Geld (amerikanisch).

3. Bei _____ Wetter soll man nicht fahren (schlecht).

4. Die Eltern haben _____ Träume (groß).

5. Trotz _____ Musik war die Party langweilig (gut).

6. Der Traktor ist aus _____ Metall (schwer).

7. Er hat nur _____ Essen (schlecht).

Comparative and superlative adjectives

16

Der Komparativ

To compare two nouns based on an attribute or characteristic, we use the comparative form of the adjective. In English we simply add *-er* or the word *more* to the adjective. For example, *this car is faster than that car*, or *this car is more beautiful than that car*. In German, it's quite simple. Unless it's a special adjective that requires special circumstances (an irregular adjective), only two things will occur. You will add **-er** to the end of the adjective, and if it has one syllable and a stem vowel of **a**, **o**, or **u**, add an umlaut.

ADJECTIVE	COMPARATIVE
alt	älter
groß	größer
häßlich	häßlicher
klein	kleiner
lockig	lockiger
lang	länger
schön	schöner

Hinweis (*Note*): If the adjective already has an umlauted vowel in its stem, nothing more needs to happen than just adding **-er** to the end.

ÜBUNG
16·1
Übersetzung (*Translation*)

1. This car is faster. _____

2. Her hair is curlier. _____

3. This house is smaller. _____

4. This stapler is older. _____

5. This pencil is longer. _____

Regelausnahmen (*Exceptions to the rule*)

Certain adjectives must be adapted before they can be used in the comparative.

Adjectives that drop a letter
hoch   höher

Adjectives that change the whole word
bald   eher
gut   besser
viel   mehr

Adjectives that do not add an umlaut
blaß
fromm
glatt
naß
rot
schmal (unusual, but possible, to take an umlaut)

Adjectives that drop the -e in -el or -er
dunkel   dunkler
teuer   teurer

ÜBUNG
16·2

Übersetzung (*Translation*)

1. The mountain is higher. _____

2. The food is better here. _____

3. I drink more water now. _____

Als, so ... wie (*Than, as . . . as*)

When making a comparison between two items, you can make an even comparison (*as tall as*) or an uneven comparison (*taller than*).

Ich bin so groß wie du. (original form of the adjective)
Ich bin größer als du. (comparative)

ÜBUNG
16·3

Lücken ausfüllen. (*Fill in the blanks.*) *Insert the correct adjective form in the blank.*

1. Das Auto ist _____ als das Fahrrad. (schnell)

2. Sie ist _____ als er. (groß)

3. Der Himmel ist so _____ wie gestern. (dunkel)

4. Der Mann spricht _____ als die Frau. (viel)

5. Der Ring ist _____ als die Uhr. (teuer)

6. Der Berg ist so _____ wie der Hügel. (hoch)

7. Das Buch ist so _____ wie die CD. (langweilig)

8. Der Stein ist so _____ wie der Baum. (alt)

Der Superlativ

The superlative is used when more than two nouns are being compared. For example, *a TV is large, a garage is larger, but a house is largest*. To form the superlative in English we say that something is *the biggest, the tallest*, or *the most beautiful*. In German you simply add -**(e)st** to the adjective's original form. In order to form the superlative when the adjective is used alone, without a noun, you add **am** before the adjective and -**(e)sten** to the end of the adjective.

ADJECTIVE	COMPARATIVE	SUPERLATIVE
alt	älter	(am) ältest(en)
groß	größer	(am) größt(en)
häßlich	häßlicher	(am) häßlichst(en)
klein	kleiner	(am) kleinst(en)
lang	länger	(am) längst(en)
lockig	lockiger	(am) lockigst(en)
schön	schöner	(am) schönst(en)

ÜBUNG
16·4

Übersetzung (Translation)

1. This car is the fastest. _____

2. Her hair is the curliest. _____

3. This house is the smallest. _____

4. This stapler is the oldest. _____

5. This pencil is the longest. _____

Regelausnahmen (*Exceptions to the rule*)

Certain adjectives must be adapted before they can be used in the superlative.

nah	näher	am nächsten
viel	mehr	am meisten

ÜBUNG

16·5

Übersetzung (*Translation*)

1. I am tall. My sister is taller. My mother is the tallest.

_____

2. The VW is expensive. The BMW is more expensive. The Audi is the most expensive.

_____

3. The bike is fast. The car is faster. The train is the fastest.

_____

4. His father is old. His uncle is older. His grandfather is the oldest.

_____

Noun phrases
Food: vegetables, fruit, meat and fish
Drinks

Die Nominalphrase (*Noun phrases*)

A simple noun phrase consists of an article and a noun. A more complex noun phrase is made up of modifiers (adjectives) in addition to the article and noun.

der Baum	*the tree*
der große alte Baum	*the big old tree*
ein großer alter Baum	*a big old tree*

Sometimes there is no article, and then the phrase is made up of just the noun or the noun and an adjective.

Sie hat Geld.	*She has money.*
Sie hat viel Geld.	*She has a lot of money.*

The adjective must always reflect the gender and case of the noun.

Der bestimmte Artikel (*The definite article*)

	MASCULINE	FEMININE	NEUTER	PLURAL
Nominative	der gute Mann	die gute Frau	das gute Ding	die guten Leute
Accusative	den guten Mann	die gute Frau	das gute Ding	die guten Leute
Dative	dem guten Mann	der guten Frau	dem guten Ding	den guten Leuten
Genitive	des guten Mannes	der guten Frau	des guten Dinges	der guten Leute

Der unbestimmte Artikel (*The indefinite article*)

	MASCULINE	FEMININE	NEUTER	PLURAL
Nominative	ein guter Mann	eine gute Frau	ein gutes Ding	gute Leute
Accusative	einen guten Mann	eine gute Frau	ein gutes Ding	gute Leute
Dative	einem guten Mann	einer guten Frau	einem guten Ding	guten Leuten
Genitive	eines guten Mannes	einer guten Frau	eines guten Dinges	guter Leute

Kein Artikel (No article)

	MASCULINE	FEMININE	NEUTER	PLURAL
Nominative	guter Mann	gute Frau	gutes Ding	gute Leute
Accusative	guten Mann	gute Frau	gutes Ding	gute Leute
Dative	gutem Mann	guter Frau	gutem Ding	guten Leuten
Genitive	guten Mannes	guter Frau	guten Dinges	guter Leute

WORTSCHATZ

Das Essen: das Gemüse (Food: vegetables)

der Blumenkohl	cauliflower	der Kopfsalat	lettuce
die Bohne	bean	der Pilz	mushroom
die Erbse	pea	der Porree	leek
die Karotte/Möhre	carrot	der Rettich	radish
die Kartoffel	potato	die Salatgurke	cucumber
der Knoblauch	garlic	die Zwiebel	onion
der Kohl	cabbage		

Das Essen: das Obst (Food: fruit)

die Ananas	pineapple	die Kirsche	cherry
der Apfel	apple	die Melone	melon
die Aprikose	apricot	die Orange	orange
die Banane	banana	der Pfirsich	peach
die Birne	pear	die Tomate	tomato
die Erdbeere	strawberry	die Traube	grape
die Grapefruit	grapefruit	die Zitrone	lemon
die Himbeere	raspberry		

Das Essen: das Fleisch/der Fisch (Food: meat/fish)

der Aufschnitt	deli meat	der Fisch	fish
die Ente	duck	die Forelle	trout
das Fleisch	meat	die Garnele	shrimp
das Geflügel	poultry	der Hering	herring
das Hähnchen	chicken	der Hummer	lobster
der Schinken	ham	die Krabbe	crab
das Schweinefleisch	pork	der Lachs	salmon
das Steak	steak	die Meeresfrüchte (pl.)	seafood

Die Getränke (Drinks)

das Bier	beer	der Saft	juice
der Kaffee	coffee	der Tee	tea
die Limonade	lemon soda	das Wasser	water
die Milch	milk	der Wein	wine
das Mineralwasser	mineral water		

ÜBUNG

17·1

Übersetzung (*Translation*). *Use the nominative case.*

1. the large house _____
2. the warm food _____
3. the small garden _____
4. the green lettuce _____
5. the cold water _____
6. the black coffee _____
7. the green banana _____
8. the juicy strawberries _____
9. the baked meat _____
10. the old apple _____

ÜBUNG

17·2

Übersetzung (*Translation*)

1. I like to eat green grapes.

   _____

2. I drink cold water after sports.

   _____

3. I don't drink coffee.

   _____

4. My mother likes to drink hot tea with milk.

   _____

5. The boys do not like to eat seafood.

   _____

6. My sister does not like to eat green grapes.

   _____

7. Do you (sing.; informal) eat a red apple every day?

   _____

8. Good children drink a lot of water.

   _____

9. They do not like to eat green eggs and cold ham.

   _____

10. I drink a tall glass of milk in the morning.

    _____

Answer the following questions using the cues given.

1. Wem schenkst du das? Das schenke ich _____. (my young cousin)

2. Was schenkst du ihr? Ich schenke ihr _____. (a new watch)

3. Wessen Haus ist das? Das ist das Haus _____. (of our old math teacher)

4. Wer besucht dich morgen? _____ besucht mich. (the German chancellor)

5. Was hast du in deiner Tasche? Ich habe _____. (five books and an ugly sweater)

6. Wohin gehst du nach der Schule? Ich gehe zu _____. (the large supermarket)

7. Wo ist die Schule? Sie ist _____ _____. (next to the small park) (in front of the beautiful castle)

Present tense
Common regular verbs

Das Präsens (*The present tense*)

The present tense is used to describe an action that occurs in the present. In English the present tense takes various forms, including the simple present and the continuous present, but in German there is only one present tense. It encompasses all of the present tenses found in English. By inserting an adverb of time, even the future can be described using the German present tense.

Die Konjugierung (*Conjugation*)

When you look up a verb in the dictionary, you will find the verb in its most basic form, the infinitive (*to* _____). The verb must then be conjugated into the correct form based on the subject who is "acting" in the sentence. The ending of the verb depends on who the subject is and how many of the subjects there are (singular vs. plural). A verb is conjugated when you drop the **-en** ending and add the correct ending for the subject. Sometimes the stem of the verb also changes. The stem is the part that comes before the verb ending.

machen	*to make, to do*
ich mache	*I make*

Weak verbs function without much deviation from the original infinitive.

Die Verbendungen (*Verb endings*)

Weak verbs are conjugated in the present tense by adding the following endings to the verb stem:

ich -e	wir -en
du -(e)st	ihr -(e)t
er -(e)t	sie -en
sie -(e)t	Sie -en
es -(e)t	

Conjugation of machen

machen *(to make, to do)*

ich mache	wir machen
du machst	ihr macht
er macht	sie machen
sie macht	Sie machen
es macht	

Sometimes an additional **-e** needs to be added before the standard ending (for **du**, **er/sie/es**, and **ihr**), but only when the verb ends in **-d**, **-t**, **-m**, or **-n**.

arbeiten
du arbeitest
er arbeitet
ihr arbeitet

Certain verbs will drop the **-s** of the ending in the **du** form, because they contain an **-s**, **-ss**, **-ß**, **-x**, or **-z** at the end of their verb stem.

heißen
du heißt

Here is a list of some common weak verbs in German, some of whose conjugation forms were already practiced in Chapter 8:

WORTSCHATZ

Common weak verbs

ändern	to change	**leben**	to live
arbeiten	to work	**lieben**	to love
atmen	to breathe	**malen**	to draw or paint
bauen	to build	**nutzen**	to use
bedeuten	to mean	**packen**	to pack
besuchen	to visit	**putzen**	to clean
bezahlen	to pay	**reisen**	to travel
bieten	to offer	**sagen**	to say
brauchen	to need	**schauen**	to look
dauern	to last	**schicken**	to send
decken	to set the table or to cover	**schmecken**	to taste
drücken	to push or press	**spazieren**	to go for a walk
erzählen	to tell	**spielen**	to play
fragen	to ask	**stören**	to bother
grüßen	to greet	**studieren**	to study
hängen	to hang	**tanzen**	to dance
heiraten	to marry	**trinken**	to drink
hören	to hear or listen	**üben**	to practice
husten	to cough	**verdienen**	to earn
jobben	to work	**verkaufen**	to sell
kaufen	to buy	**wandern**	to hike
kochen	to cook	**wechseln**	to exchange or change
kosten	to cost	**wohnen**	to live
kriegen	to get (slang)	**zahlen**	to pay
lachen	to laugh	**zeigen**	to show or point out

Übersetzung (*Translation*)

1. We are building a house. _____

2. The girl is studying German. _____

3. They pay (the bill). _____

4. You (pl., informal) exchange your money. _____

5. He lives in Germany. _____

6. We dance the waltz. _____

7. The food tastes good. _____

8. My children practice their music. _____

9. My mother is hiking. _____

10. I cook and travel. _____

Was machst du? (*What do you do?*) *What would you do in the following situations?*

1. Ich habe einen Herd. _____

2. Ich höre einen Witz (*a joke*). _____

3. Mein Hals kratzt (*feels itchy*). _____

4. Ich bin bei meiner Oma. _____

5. Ich habe einen Koffer und meine Kleidung. _____

6. Ich bin im Flugzeug. _____

7. Ich liebe meinen Partner. _____

8. Ich kann aus den Fenstern nicht sehen. _____

9. Ich arbeite. _____

10. Ich bin in Europa und habe amerikanische Dollar. _____

Verbkategorien (*Verb categories*)

German verbs are divided into three categories: weak, strong, and mixed verbs. The stem vowel does not change with weak verbs, and they are what we are practicing in this chapter. Other verbs—namely, strong and mixed verbs—act differently. These verbs will be studied in more detail in the following chapters.

Categorizing verbs helps especially when forming the past tense of the verb. This will be studied in Chapters 28, 29, and 30.

Another way that verbs can be categorized is by special conditions that apply. For example, some verbs may begin with what is called a separable or inseparable prefix (Chapter 20).

Irregular verbs (strong verbs)

Das starke Verb (*Strong verbs*)

German verbs are divided into three categories: weak, strong, and mixed verbs. The previous chapter (18) dealt with weak verbs, where the stem vowel did not change. Here we look at the strong verb, which is a type of irregular verb.

The present tense of the strong verb is unpredictable. Each verb changes in its own way; however, all verbs change in a similar pattern—in that the stem vowel may change in the present, but will definitely change in the past tense. (The past tense will be discussed in Chapters 28, 29, and 30.)

Die Konjugierung starker Verben (*The conjugation of strong verbs*)

Like the regular verbs, irregular verbs share the same verb endings, except that you do not need to add an extra -e before the verb ending (this only applies to **du**, **er**, **sie**, and **es** as well as **ihr**). However, sometimes the stem vowel changes. This occurs in the **du** and **er/sie/es** forms. Stems with an **a** change it to an **ä**, and stems with an **e** change it to either **i** or **ie**, depending on whether the stem vowel is followed by one or multiple consonants.

tragen (*to wear*)	
du trägst	*you wear*
er/sie/es trägt	*he/she/it wears*
essen (*to eat*)	
du isst	*you eat*
er/sie/es isst	*he/she/it eats*

There are only a few words that are affected by this rule. All other verbs function similarly to the regular verbs.

Konjugierung (*Conjugation*). *Write the correct forms of the second and third person singular in the blanks provided.*

	DU	ER/SIE/ES
1. fangen (*to catch*)	_____	_____
2. brechen (*to break*)	_____	_____
3. empfehlen (*to recommend*)	_____	_____
4. essen (*to eat*)	_____	_____
5. geben (*to give*)	_____	_____
6. lassen (*to let, allow*)	_____	_____
7. lesen (*to read*)	_____	_____
8. nehmen (*to take*)	_____	_____
9. schlafen (*to sleep*)	_____	_____
10. sehen (*to see*)	_____	_____

WORTSCHATZ

Common irregular verbs

backen	to bake	**heben**	to lift or raise
bekommen	to get or receive	**heißen**	to be called or named
bitten	to ask for	**kommen**	to come
bleiben	to stay or remain	**reiten**	to ride a horse
bringen	to bring	**schreiben**	to write
empfinden	to feel	**schwimmen**	to swim
finden	to find	**singen**	to sing
fliegen	to fly	**trinken**	to drink
gehen	to go	**verlieren**	to lose

ÜBUNG
19·2

Übersetzung (*Translation*)

1. My name is Svenja. _____

2. They drink milk. _____

3. We are staying here. _____

4. The bird is flying. _____

5. You (sing., informal) come from Florida. _____

6. He catches the ball. _____

7. My mother is writing a letter. _____

Separable- and inseparable-prefix verbs

Das Präfix (*Prefixes*)

A prefix is a combination of letters that when added to the beginning of a word can change the meaning of the word. In German, there are two types of prefixes: separable and inseparable prefixes. These prefixes sometimes substantially change the meaning of the verb. There are many prefixes and they are used often, which makes it more challenging to the learner.

These prefixes are not limited to German. In fact, English uses a similar structure quite frequently. Take this example:

> to give
> to give in, to give up, to give out

Although the meaning of *to give* is *to grant someone something*, *to give up* means *to quit*. Simply by adding the preposition *up*, one changes the entire meaning.

Das trennbare Präfix (*Separable prefixes*)

The following prefixes are considered separable prefixes and theoretically have their own functions when not accompanying the verb. Here are a few of the separable prefixes.

ab	*ex, from*	ein	*in*
an	*about, on, against*	mit	*with*
auf	*on top of, up*	vor	*before, in front of, from*
aus	*out of, from*	weg	*away, off*
bei	*at, by, near*	zusammen	*together*

Separable prefixes separate from their verbs in most cases; however, when the separable-prefix verb finds itself in the infinitive form, in subordinating dependent clauses, or when functioning as a past participle, the prefix stays attached to the verb. In other cases, the regularly conjugated verb is placed in the second position of the sentence (statements) and the prefix is "kicked" to the end and placed immediately before the period at the end of the sentence.

abfliegen	*to take off by plane*
Ich fliege ab.	*I am taking off.*
Ich fliege morgen ab.	*I am taking off tomorrow.*
Ich fliege morgen um sieben Uhr ab.	*I am taking off tomorrow at seven o'clock.*

| Ich fliege morgen um sieben Uhr mit Lufthansa ab. | I am taking off tomorrow at seven o'clock with Lufthansa. |
| Ich fliege morgen um sieben Uhr mit Lufthansa von Chicago ab. | I am taking off from Chicago tomorrow at seven o'clock with Lufthansa. |

It does not matter how long the sentence is, the separable prefix will still go to the very end unless it is connected to the verb, in one of the three structures described above.

Ich muss morgen abfliegen.	I must take off tomorrow.
Weißt du, dass ich morgen abfliege?	Did you know that I am taking off tomorrow?
Ich bin gestern abgeflogen.	I took off yesterday.

ÜBUNG
20·1

Lücken ausfüllen. (Fill in the blanks.) *Fill in the blanks with the correct parts of each separable-prefix verb.*

1. (abfliegen) Wann _____ du am Donnerstag _____?

2. (austrinken) Wir _____ unseren Wein _____.

3. (aufessen) Er _____ alles vom Teller _____.

4. (mitnehmen) Was _____ Sie auf die Reise _____?

5. (einleben) Ich _____ mich in dem neuen Haus _____.

6. (anprobieren) Hans _____ die neue Hose _____.

7. (mitkommen) _____ die Hannelore _____?

ÜBUNG
20·2

Satzbausteine. *Create sentences using the following cues.*

1. um acht Uhr / anfangen / die Schule

_____

2. gut / die Schuhe / aussehen

_____

3. pünktlich / der Zug / ankommen / nicht

_____

4. mir / einfallen / nichts

_____

5. meine Eltern / mitfahren / im Auto

_____

6. die Schüler / wegfahren / als Klasse / in die Schweiz

_____

7. der Vater / zudecken / das schlafende Kind

_____

Das untrennbare Präfix (*Inseparable prefixes*)

The following prefixes are considered inseparable prefixes and cannot function without a verb. Here are a few of the inseparable prefixes:

be-	makes a verb transitive (requires a direct object) or means going toward the object
emp-	can make a verb out of a noun or mean going away
ent-	functions just like **emp-**
er-	adds an umlaut to the stem vowel or means becoming something
ge-	completion of an action
miss-	functions just like English *mis-*, shows lack of success
ver-	completion or going away or misguiding
zer-	apart, separate, or destroy

ÜBUNG
20·3

Satzbausteine. *Create sentences using the following cues.*

1. die Schüler / beantworten / die Frage

_____

2. wir / die Anleitung / nicht / verstehen

_____

3. versagen / das Auto / in der Wüste

_____

4. der Lehrer / vergessen / die Aufgaben / zu Hause

_____

5. versprechen / die Eltern / nichts

_____

Grammar

Vocabulary

Fun facts

The irregular verb haben Animals

·21·

In addition to strong verbs, there are a few verbs that are considered to be irregular. The verb **haben** (*to have*) is one of them. **Haben** is a very common verb, and it is especially vital in forming the conversational past/present perfect, which is covered in Chapter 28.

Die Konjugierung von haben
(*The conjugation of* to have)

haben (*to have*)	
ich habe	wir haben
du hast	ihr habt
er hat	sie haben
sie hat	Sie haben
es hat	

Note that for the second and third person singular forms, the **b** is taken out of the stem before the **du** and **er/sie/es** verb endings are added.

To say that you *don't have* something, simply add **nicht** to the end of the sentence, or replace the indefinite article with **kein**.

Ich habe kein Haus.   *I don't have a house. (Literally: I have no house.)*

ÜBUNG
21·1

Lücken ausfüllen. (*Fill in the blanks.*) *Fill in each blank with the correct form of* **haben**.

1. Ich _____ morgen eine Matheprüfung.

2. _____ wir etwas zu trinken?

3. Mein Vater und meine Mutter _____ ein eigenes Haus.

4. Der Hans _____ ein neues Auto.

5. _____ ihr das Buch von Harry Potter?

6. Frau Schmitt, _____ Sie einen Kuli?

7. Du _____ viel zu lernen.

Die Tiere (*Animals*)

bear	**der Bär**	kangaroo	**das Känguru**
bird	**der Vogel**	lamb	**der Lamm**
bull	**der Stier**	lion	**der Löwe**
cat	**die Katze**	monkey	**der Affe**
chicken	**das Huhn**	mouse	**die Maus**
cow	**die Kuh**	pig	**das Schwein**
dog	**der Hund**	rabbit	**der Hase**
donkey	**der Esel**	rat	**die Ratte**
duck	**die Ente**	rooster	**der Hahn**
elephant	**der Elefant**	sheep	**der Schaf**
fish	**der Fisch**	tiger	**der Tiger**
fox	**der Fuchs**	tomcat	**der Kater**
frog	**der Frosch**	turkey	**der Truthahn**
horse	**das Pferd**	wolf	**der Wolf**

ÜBUNG

21·2

Übersetzung (*Translation*)

1. I have a horse. _____

2. I don't have a wolf. _____

3. We have two cats. _____

4. My sister doesn't have a chicken. _____

5. They have some dogs. _____

6. You (pl., informal) have ducks. _____

7. He doesn't have mice. _____

8. Mrs. Thomas, you have a fish. _____

ÜBUNG
21·3

Wo ist das Tier? (*Where is the animal?*) *Place an X in the column where you would most likely find each of the animals listed below:* **zu Hause** (at home), **im Zoo** (at the zoo), *or* **auf dem Bauernhof** (on the farm).

	(H) ZU HAUSE	(Z) IM ZOO	(B) AUF DEM BAUERNHOF
1. das Känguru	_____	_____	_____
2. der Affe	_____	_____	_____
3. der Vogel	_____	_____	_____
4. das Huhn	_____	_____	_____
5. der Löwe	_____	_____	_____
6. der Hund	_____	_____	_____
7. der Truthahn	_____	_____	_____
8. der Fisch	_____	_____	_____
9. das Pferd	_____	_____	_____
10. das Schwein	_____	_____	_____
11. die Katze	_____	_____	_____
12. die Kuh	_____	_____	_____
13. der Hahn	_____	_____	_____

Spaßfakten (*Fun facts*)

Deutschland und Tiere (*Germany and animals*)

Es gibt fast 700 zoologische Gärten, Wildparks, Aquarien, Vogelparks und Tierreservate in Deutschland.

Es gibt 414 Tiergärten.

Der Berliner Zoologischer Garten ist mit 1500 verschiedenen Tierarten und 14.000 Tieren der Weltgrößte.

Schäferhunde haben die besten Hundenasen und werden deswegen als Polizeihund trainiert. Warum die gute Nase? Sie haben 225 Million Zellrezeptoren in ihren Nasen.

Der Schäferhund hütete (*herded*) ursprünglich Tiergruppen.

Der erste Mann, der einen Schäferhund züchtete (*bred*), war Max von Stephanitz. Der erste Welpe (*puppy*) der zweiten Generation war Beowulf, der Stammvater aller Schäferhunde. Der Schäferhund wurde erst 1899 zum ersten Mal gezüchtet.

Eine kurze Weile hieß der Schäferhund auf Englisch *Alsatian*, weil es nach dem zweiten Weltkrieg Probleme mit dem Namen „Deutschen" Schäferhund gab.

The irregular verb **sein** Professions

The verb **sein** (introduced briefly in Chapter 15) is an irregular verb, and once one sees its conjugation, it is easy to understand why. Not a single conjugated form of the verb looks like the original infinitive. Like **haben**, it is a very common verb and refers to the state of anything; the object of **sein** can easily replace the subject, as they are one and the same. Again like **haben**, **sein** is used to form the conversational past and is therefore extremely common.

Ich bin Lehrerin.	*I am a teacher.*
Er ist müde.	*He is tired.*

Die Konjugierung von sein (*The conjugation of to be*)

sein (*to be*)	
ich bin	wir sind
du bist	ihr seid
er ist	sie sind
sie ist	Sie sind
es ist	

ÜBUNG
22·1

Lücken ausfüllen. (*Fill in the blanks.*) *Fill in each blank with the correct form of the verb* **sein**.

1. Wir _____ eine Familie.

2. Er _____ Schüler.

3. Das _____ eine Bank.

4. Wo _____ meine Schuhe?

5. Der Mann _____ mein Mann.

6. Herr Thomas, was _____ Sie vom Beruf?

7. Silke und du _____ meine besten Freunde.

Die Berufe (*Professions*)

	MASCULINE	FEMININE
businessperson	der Geschäftsmann	die Geschäftsfrau
dentist	der Zahnarzt	die Zahnärztin
doctor, physician	der Arzt	die Ärztin
electrician	der Elektriker	die Elektrikerin
farmer	der Bauer	die Bäuerin
lawyer, attorney	der Anwalt	die Anwältin
musician	der Musiker	die Musikerin
nurse	der Krankenpfleger	die Krankenschwester
plumber	der Klempner	die Klempnerin
police officer	der Polizist	die Polizistin
politician	der Politiker	die Politikerin
principal	der Schulleiter	die Schulleiterin
professor	der Professor	die Professorin
salesperson	der Kaufmann	die Kauffrau
singer	der Sänger	die Sängerin
stay-at-home parent, homemaker	der Hausmann	die Hausfrau
teacher	der Lehrer	die Lehrerin
truck driver	der LKW-Fahrer	die LKW-Fahrerin
waitperson	der Kellner	die Kellnerin
writer	der Autor	die Autorin

ÜBUNG
22·2

Stimmt das oder stimmt es nicht? (*True or false?*) *Mark each of the following statements as true (**S**) or false (**SN**). Note that there is no indefinite article before a profession in German.*

1. _____ Harry Potter ist Professor.

2. _____ Donald Trump ist Geschäftsmann.

3. _____ Micky Maus und Minni Maus sind Krankenschwester.

4. _____ Kaufmänner und Kauffrauen arbeiten bei Sears.

5. _____ Die Rolling Stones sind Musiker.

6. _____ Madonna ist LKW-Fahrerin.

7. _____ Stephen King ist Autor.

8. _____ Angela Merkel ist Politikerin.

Übersetzung (*Translation*)

1. I am an electrician. _____

2. She is a police officer. _____

3. He is a stay-at-home dad. _____

4. We are teachers. _____

5. You all (pl., informal) are doctors. _____

6. They are plumbers. _____

Werden
Future tense
More professions

Werden (Will, *future tense*)

Unlike its cohorts, **haben** and **sein**, **werden** is used to form the future tense and can also be used to form the passive tense. It denotes what will happen at a point in time not yet present. It follows a similar conjugation pattern to that of **haben**, where the second and third person singular forms change their stem ending. In addition, **werden** belongs to the category of stem-vowel-changing verbs, meaning that because there is an **e** in the stem, the **du** and **er/sie/es** forms will change to an **i** in their stem.

Das Futur (*The future tense*)

Because the future can be expressed by using the present along with an adverb of time, the verb **werden** is not used as consistently as the verb *will* in English. **Werden** sends the meaning-carrying verb that it accompanies to the end of the sentence, in the infinitive form.

When **werden** is used to explain what profession one will practice, no second infinitive verb is used. In that context, **werden** means *will become*. This also applies to descriptions of the weather (**Es wird heiß.** *It's getting hot.*) and changes of state (**Wasser wird Eis.** *Water turns into ice.*).

werden *(will)*	
ich werde	wir werden
du wirst	ihr werdet
er wird	sie werden
sie wird	Sie werden
es wird	

ÜBUNG
23·1

Lücken ausfüllen. (*Fill in the blanks.*) *Fill in each blank with the correct form of the verb* **werden**.

1. Sie (pl.) _____ das Haus kaufen.

2. Die Schüler _____ morgen zu Hause bleiben.

3. Ich _____ Pilot.

4. Meine Frau _____ nächste Woche ein Kind bekommen.

5. _____ ihr eine Frage stellen?

6. Herr Becker, _____ Sie ein Auto fahren?

7. _____ du auch müde?

WORTSCHATZ

Mehr Berufe (More Professions)

	MASCULINE	FEMININE
accountant	der Buchhalter	die Buchhalterin
actor	der Schauspieler	die Schauspielerin
architect	der Architekt	die Architektin
bus driver	der Busfahrer	die Busfahrerin
butcher	der Metzger	die Metzgerin
carpenter	der Tischler	die Tischlerin
chemist	der Chemiker	die Chemikerin
cook	der Koch	die Köchin
dancer	der Tänzer	die Tänzerin
firefighter	der Feuerwehrmann	die Feuerwehrfrau
gardener	der Gärtner	die Gärtnerin
jeweler	der Juwelier	die Juwelierin
journalist	der Journalist	die Journalistin
judge	der Richter	die Richterin
librarian	der Bibliothekar	die Bibliothekarin
mail/letter carrier	der Briefträger	die Briefträgerin
mechanic	der Mechaniker	die Mechanikerin
pharmacist	der Apotheker	die Apothekerin
reporter	der Reporter	die Reporterin
scientist	der Wissenschaftler	die Wissenschaftlerin
spy	der Spion	die Spionin
taxi driver	der Taxifahrer	die Taxifahrerin
veterinarian	der Tierarzt	die Tierärztin

ÜBUNG
23·2

Welcher Beruf? (Which profession?) *Write the name of the profession after each description or name.*

1. Ein Arzt, der mit Tieren arbeitet: _____

2. Eine Frau, die die Medikamente organisiert: _____

3. James Bond: _____

4. Diese Frau kocht gutes Essen im Café: _____

5. Er arbeitet gern mit Blumen (*flowers*): _____

6. Diesen Mann sehen wir in einem Hollywood-Film: _____

Stimmt das oder stimmt es nicht? (*True or false?*) *Mark each sentence true (**S**) or false (**SN**).*

1. _____ Vijay Singh ist Golfspieler.

2. _____ Julia Roberts ist Apothekerin.

3. _____ Fred Astaire ist Tänzer.

4. _____ Wolfgang Puck ist Koch.

5. _____ Angelina Jolie ist Schmuckmacherin.

6. _____ Heidi Klum ist Architektin.

7. _____ Til Schweiger ist Tischler.

8. _____ Sonia Sotomayor ist Richterin.

Übersetzung (*Translation*)

1. You (pl., informal) will all be firefighters. _____

2. They will be gardeners. _____

3. She will be a butcher. _____

4. He will be a journalist. _____

5. I will be a spy. _____

6. You (sing., informal) will be a veterinarian. _____

7. We will be mechanics. _____

8. I will become a chef. _____

Helping verbs (modal auxiliaries)

Das Modalhilfsverb (*The modal auxiliary or helping verb*)

A helping verb, or modal verb, is an action word that assists the main verb or main meaning-carrying verb in the sentence. These helping verbs all function as irregular verbs and can be conjugated in a very similar way. Modals must work together with another verb, and that verb is moved to the end of the sentence, in the infinitive form. There are six of these modal verbs.

	mögen to like	dürfen to be allowed (to)	können to be able (to)	müssen to have to	wollen to want (to)	sollen should
ich	mag	darf	kann	muss	will	soll
du	magst	darfst	kannst	musst	willst	sollst
er/sie/es	mag	darf	kann	muss	will	soll
wir	mögen	dürfen	können	müssen	wollen	sollen
ihr	mögt	dürft	könnt	müsst	wollt	sollt
sie/Sie	mögen	dürfen	können	müssen	wollen	sollen

> Wir mögen den Film.
> Darf ich bitte einen Bleistift haben?
> Sie kann nicht Fahrrad fahren. Sie ist nur drei Jahre alt.
> Musst du deine Hausaufgabe machen?
> Er will ins Kino gehen, aber er hat kein Geld.
> Sie soll den Tisch decken.

Hinweis (*Note*): The **wir** and **sie/Sie** forms of the modals are identical to the infinitive form, and the **ich** and **er/sie/es** forms are identical to each other. In the singular, there is usually a vowel change, except in **sollen**, where every form keeps the stem **soll**.

Mögen

The conjugation shown above for **mögen** is correct for when **mögen** is used alone. However, when combining it with a second verb, the subjunctive form **möchten** is used.

möchten *(subjunctive of **mögen**)*	
ich möchte	wir möchten
du möchtest	ihr möchtet
er/sie/es möchte	sie/Sie möchten

Übersetzung (*Translation*)

1. My family wants to build a house.

   _____

2. Her sister is not allowed to drive a car.

   _____

3. The man is not able to hear.

   _____

4. We should cook supper.

   _____

5. You (sing., informal) must do your homework.

   _____

6. It would like to eat something. [*It is an animal.*]

   _____

7. Are you (pl., informal) allowed to go to the movies?

   _____

Wissen and kennen
In the city

·25·

Wissen, which means *to know a fact*, is also an irregular verb, and it is conjugated just like a modal auxiliary verb. However, **wissen** must be followed by a dependent, subordinating clause. Some examples of words that introduce such clauses are **dass** (*that*) and any of the question words.

Die Konjugierung von wissen
(*The conjugation of* to know [*a fact*])

wissen (*to know*)	
ich weiß	wir wissen
du weißt	ihr wisst
er/sie/es weiß	sie/Sie wissen

Ich weiß nicht, wann der Zug kommt.	*I don't know when the train will arrive.*
Wir wissen nicht, dass der Laden zu ist.	*We don't know that the store is closed.*

WORTSCHATZ

In der Stadt (*In the city*)

zum/zur	to the	**die Informationsstelle**	information counter
der Bahnhof	train station	**die Innenstadt**	downtown
die Bank	bank	**die Kirche**	church
die Bushaltestelle	bus stop	**der Marktplatz**	market square
die Fußgängerzone	pedestrian zone	**das Museum**	museum
das Hotel	hotel	**die U-Bahn-Station**	subway station

Lücken ausfüllen. (*Fill in the blanks.*) *Fill in each blank with the correct form of* **wissen**.

1. _____ du, wann der Zug kommt?

2. _____ ihr, wie ich zum Bahnhof komme?

3. _____ Sie, wo das Museum ist?

4. _____ er, wann die Informationsstelle auf ist?

5. _____ wir, wie wir zur Bushaltestelle kommen?

6. _____ die Sonja, wo der Markt ist?

WORTSCHATZ

Artifakten	artifacts	**Kunst**	art
bekommen	to get/obtain	**mit dem Zug**	with the train
der Turm	tower/steeple	**schlafen**	to sleep
fahren	to drive/ride	**sehen**	to see
kaufen	to buy	**zu Hause**	at home

Stimmt das oder stimmt es nicht? (*True or false?*) *Mark each sentence true (**S**) or false (**SN**).*

1. _____ Man fährt mit dem Zug.

2. _____ Man sieht im Museum Artifakten und Kunst.

3. _____ Man kauft den Bahnhof.

4. _____ Eine Kirche ist sehr groß und hat einen Turm.

5. _____ In der Bank bekommt man Bananen.

6. _____ Ein Hotel ist wo man schlafen kann, wenn man nicht zu Hause ist.

ÜBUNG
25·3

Worüber wissen diese Personen viel? (*About what do these people know a lot?*) *Match each person to the appropriate area of expertise.*

1. _____ Eine Apothekerin weiß viel über

2. _____ Ein Tänzer weiß viel über

3. _____ Tischler wissen viel über

4. _____ Wissenschaftler wissen viel über

5. _____ Ein Koch weiß viel über

6. _____ Die Metzgerin weiß viel über

A. Essen.

B. Fleisch (*meat*).

C. den Körper.

D. Holz und Werkzeuge (*wood and tools*).

E. Medizin.

F. Theorie.

Die Konjugierung von kennen (*The conjugation of to know [familiarity]*)

Kennen also means *to know,* but in this case it is about familiarity with a noun. The verb **kennen** is always followed by a direct object.

kennen (*to know*)	
ich kenne	wir kennen
du kennst	ihr kennt
er/sie/es kennt	sie/Sie kennen

Sie kennt meinen Namen.
Wir kennen Berlin.

She knows my name.
We are familiar with Berlin.

ÜBUNG
25·4

Stimmt das oder stimmt es nicht? (*True or false?*) *Mark each sentence true (**S**) or false (**SN**).*

1. _____ Ich kenne meine Freunde.

2. _____ Brad Pitt kennt Angelina Jolie.

3. _____ Jay Leno kennt viele Schauspieler.

4. _____ Anakin Skywalker kennt Romeo und Juliet.

5. _____ Barack Obama kennt Angela Merkel nicht.

6. _____ Hillary Clinton kennt Washington, D.C.

7. _____ Steven Spielberg kennt Hollywood nicht.

Übersetzung (*Translation*)

1. I know a few people. _____

2. My electrician knows my husband. _____

3. Our veterinarian knows many families. _____

4. We know Seattle very well. _____

5. He knows the students. _____

Kennen vs. wissen

Again, both of these verbs mean *to know*; just keep in mind that they correspond to different meanings of the verb *to know*.

> Ich weiß, wer er ist. = Ich kenne ihn.
> *I know who he is. = I know him.*

·VI·

Grammar

Vocabulary

Fun facts

Reflexive verbs

26

Reflexivverben (*Reflexive verbs*)

The reflexive verb (**das Reflexivverb**) is used when the subject and the object are the same, and when an activity is done to oneself.

Ich wasche das Auto.	*I wash the car.*

But:

Ich wasche mich.	*I wash myself.*

WORTSCHATZ

Reflexivverben (*Reflexive verbs*)

Akkusativ

sich amüsieren	to amuse oneself	**sich freuen auf** + AKK	to look forward to
sich aufregen (**über** + AKK)	to get upset (about)	**sich gewöhnen an** + AKK	to get used to
sich beeilen	to hurry	**sich interessieren für** + AKK	to be interested in
sich beklagen	to complain	**sich kümmern um** + AKK	to watch out for / to take care of
sich benehmen	to behave	**sich umsehen**	to look around
sich entscheiden	to decide	**sich umziehen**	to change clothing
sich entschuldigen	to excuse oneself / to apologize	**sich unterhalten**	to entertain oneself
sich erholen	to relax	**sich verspäten**	to be late or delayed
sich erinnern (**an** + AKK)	to remind or remember (something)	**sich vorstellen**	to introduce oneself
sich erkälten	to catch a cold	**sich wundern** (**über** + AKK)	to be be surprised (about)

Dativ

sich fürchten vor + DAT	to be afraid of
sich vorstellen	to imagine
sich weh tun	to hurt oneself

Akkusativ oder Dativ

sich rasieren	to shave oneself / a part of one's body
sich setzen	to sit down
sich verletzten	to injure oneself / a part of one's body
sich waschen	to wash oneself / a part of one's body

Conjugate the following verbs using the correct reflexive forms.

	ICH	DU	ER/SIE/ES	WIR	IHR	SIE/SIE
1. erholen	_____	_____	_____	_____	_____	_____
2. waschen	_____	_____	_____	_____	_____	_____
3. vorstellen	_____	_____	_____	_____	_____	_____
4. rasieren	_____	_____	_____	_____	_____	_____
5. verspäten	_____	_____	_____	_____	_____	_____
6. erkälten	_____	_____	_____	_____	_____	_____
7. beeilen	_____	_____	_____	_____	_____	_____
8. setzen	_____	_____	_____	_____	_____	_____
9. entscheiden	_____	_____	_____	_____	_____	_____
10. weh tun	_____	_____	_____	_____	_____	_____

Übersetzung (*Translation*)

1. We amuse ourselves every weekend. _____

2. They sit down. _____

3. He shaves every morning. _____

4. You (pl., informal) will catch a cold! _____

5. Mr. Sturm, you should relax. _____

6. She must decide now. _____

7. You (sing., informal) are hurting your leg. _____

8. I cannot hurry. _____

9. They must get dressed. _____

Build sentences out of the following cues. Remember to change the verb ending and use the correct reflexive pronoun. Also, don't forget to choose appropriately between accusative and dative!

1. Sam / sich beeilen / jeden Morgen _____

2. Wir / sich interessieren / für Sport _____

3. Er / sich entschuldigen / bei mir _____

4. Das Kind / sich fürchten vor / der Sturm _____

5. Die Kinder / sich waschen _____

6. Ihr / sich waschen / die Gesichter _____

7. Ich / sich aufregen / über meine schlechte Note _____

Spaßfakten (*Fun facts*)

Die Körperpflege (*Personal hygiene*)

- Die Deutschen duschen sich nicht immer jeden Tag.
- Der Körpergeruch ist etwas Natürliches, nicht etwas Schlechtes.
- Manche ältere Frauen rasieren sich weder die Beine noch die Achselhöhlen.
- Man geht oft nackt in deutsche Saunen.
- Wenn man beim Arzt ist, zieht man sich komplett aus, aber der Arzt bleibt die ganze Zeit im Zimmer!

Imperative verbs (commands) Food and drink again

27

Die Befehlsform (*The imperative*)

The imperative verb form (**die Befehlsform**) is used to give a command (requesting information, following instructions, etc.). The form of the verb is determined by how many people are being commanded, and who they are. A command can be given to one person or be meant to include other people.

Du

To form the singular familiar (**du**) command for *you*, simply take the verb ending -**en** off of the regular infinitive verb and leave only the stem. If the verb is irregular, observe the stem-vowel change and/or place the separable prefix at the end of the phrase. If the stem has an umlaut, remove it.

hören	Hör die Musik! (*Listen to the music!*)
aufhören	Hör auf! (*Stop!*)
tragen	Trag das Kleid zum Ball! (*Wear the dress to the dance!*)
essen	Iss den Teller leer! (*Eat everything on your plate!*)
geben	Gib mir das Papier! (*Give me the paper!*)

Ihr

To form the plural familiar (**ihr**) command for *you*, take the stem and add a -**t**. The form looks identical to the **ihr**-form of the verb, but there is no subject.

hören	Hört die Musik! (*Listen to the music!*)
aufhören	Hört auf! (Stop!)
tragen	Tragt das Kleid zum Ball! (*Wear the dress to the dance!*)
essen	Esst den Teller leer! (*Eat everything on your plates!*)
geben	Gebt mir das Papier! (*Give me the paper!*)

Sie

To form the formal (singular and plural) (**Sie**) command for *you*, take the infinitive form and follow it with **Sie**.

hören	Hören Sie die Musik! (*Listen to the music!*)
aufhören	Hören Sie auf! (*Stop!*)
tragen	Tragen Sie das Kleid zum Ball! (*Wear the dress to the dance!*)

essen	Essen Sie den Teller leer! (*Eat everything on your plate[s]!*)
geben	Geben Sie mir das Papier! (*Give me the paper!*)

It is always more polite to include a friendly **bitte** to take away the harsh tone of a demand.

Wir

The **wir** command is different. Instead of issuing a command to one or more other people, this command form includes the speaker. The English equivalent would be *Let's . . .* and an activity that the speaker suggests all included do.

To form the **wir**-inclusive command, simply follow the pattern of the formal command. Omit **Sie** and add **wir**.

hören	Hören wir die Musik! (*Let's listen to the music!*)
aufhören	Hören wir auf! (*Let's stop!*)
tragen	Tragen wir etwas Schönes zum Ball! (*Let's wear something nice to the dance!*)
essen	Essen wir die Teller leer! (*Let's eat everything on our plates!*)
geben	Geben wir ihm das Papier! (*Let's give him the paper!*)

ÜBUNG
27·1

Change the following regular sentences to commands.

1. Du machst die Hausaufgabe. _____

2. Wir schenken ihr einen Blumenstrauß. _____

3. Ihr holt ein Buch aus der Bibliothek. _____

4. Wir fahren in die Stadt. _____

5. Sie kaufen einen neuen Wagen. _____

6. Du gehst in die Schule. _____

7. Wir sehen einen Film. _____

8. Sie nehmen die Klasse mit. _____

9. Ihr geht ins Kino. _____

10. Du schläfst ein. _____

Das Essen (*Food*)

bread	das Brot	ham	der Schinken
broccoli	der Brokkoli	meat	das Fleisch
carrot	die Möhre	onion	die Zwiebel
cheese	der Käse	potato	die Kartoffel
corn	der Mais	sausage	die Wurst
egg	das Ei	vegetables	das Gemüse
fruit	das Obst		

Die Getränke (*Beverages*)

coffee	der Kaffee	milk	die Milch
cola	die Cola	water	das (Mineral)wasser
juice	der Saft		

Wo man die kauft (*Where to buy them*)

at the supermarket	im Supermarkt
at the butcher's	beim Metzger
at the baker's	beim Bäcker
at the fruit and vegetable stand	im Obst- und Gemüseladen

Wann man die kauft (*When to buy them*)

zum Frühstück	for breakfast
zum Mittag	for lunch
zum Abendessen	for dinner

ÜBUNG
27·2

Übersetzung (*Translation*)

1. (du) Buy the bread at the baker's. _____

2. (ihr) Fetch the meat at the butcher's. _____

3. (Sie) Ask that man. _____

4. (Sie) Give me the pen. _____

5. (wir) Let's buy the milk at the supermarket. _____

6. (wir) Let's begin. _____

7. (du) Drink a little water. _____

8. (ihr) Don't drink coffee. _____

ÜBUNG 27·3

Wann isst man das? (*When do you eat that?*) *Mark an X for each meal during which you would typically eat the foods listed below:* **zum Frühstück** *(breakfast),* **zum Mittag** *(lunch) oder* **zum Abendessen** *(dinner).*

	FRÜHSTÜCK (F)	MITTAG (M)	ABENDESSEN (A)
1. das Brot	_____	_____	_____
2. der Mais	_____	_____	_____
3. das Gemüse	_____	_____	_____
4. die Wurst	_____	_____	_____
5. die Milch	_____	_____	_____
6. der Kaffee	_____	_____	_____
7. das Ei	_____	_____	_____

The imperative form of sein

The imperative form of **sein** is a special case. The stem is **sei-** (the endings stay the same).

ÜBUNG 27·4

Lücken ausfüllen. (*Fill in the blanks.*) *Put the correct form of* **sein** *in each blank.*

1. _____ Sie ruhig!

2. _____ glücklich! (du)

3. _____ wir doch klar!

4. _____ pünktlich! (ihr)

5. _____ mir bitte nicht böse! (du)

6. _____ Sie nett!

The present perfect Activities around the house

Das Perfekt (*The conversational past or present perfect*)

The conversational past tense (**das Perfekt**), also called the present perfect, describes events that occurred in the past. In German, it is used predominantly in speech, and it is only used in written texts when it functions as a direct quote.

The present perfect is made up of two parts: a helping verb (**haben** or **sein**) and the past participle, which is placed at the end of the sentence.

to buy	kaufen	hat gekauft	*bought*
to be	sein	ist gewesen	*was*

It is relatively easy to figure out whether to use **haben** or **sein** for any given verb. If the verb takes a direct object, it usually uses **haben**. If the verb shows a change of state or a change of place, it uses **sein**. Again, there may be exceptions to this rule; however, this rule of thumb is usually correct.

The participle formation is determined by the strength of the verb. Weak verbs usually end in **-t**, strong verbs in **-en**, and mixed verbs have a stem-vowel change and end in -**t**. The only way to know what the participles look like is to memorize them.

Formation of past participles

Past participles of weak verbs

Past participles of weak verbs usually look like the **er/sie/es** form with a **ge-** in front.

fragen	gefragt
machen	gemacht
spielen	gespielt

If a verb ends in -**ieren** or begins with an inseparable prefix, no **ge-** is added to the front.

manipulieren	manipuliert
studieren	studiert
erzählen	erzählt
verdienen	verdient

In the majority of cases, **haben** will be the helping verb.

Ich habe ein Auto gekauft.   *I bought a car.*
Sie hat Deutsch studiert.   *She studied German.*

Past participles of strong verbs

Strong verbs are not so easy. Sometimes they may seem to follow the same pattern as similar English words.

sing   has sung   singen   hat gesungen

Sometimes they may look completely different from the infinitive. They may even have a stem-vowel change.

be   has been   sein   ist gewesen

The easiest thing is simply to memorize each of these verbs.

Past participles of mixed verbs

Mixed verbs are a mix of weak (**ge_____t**) and strong (stem-vowel change). There are relatively few of these. Because there are so few, they are all listed here:

brennen	hat gebrannt	*to burn*
bringen	hat gebracht	*to bring*
denken	hat gedacht	*to think*
kennen	hat gekannt	*to know*
nennen	hat genannt	*to name*
rennen	ist gerannt	*to run*
senden	hat gesandt	*to send*
wenden	hat gewandt	*to turn*
wissen	hat gewusst	*to know*

WORTSCHATZ

Im Haus (*Activities around the house*)

to bake	**backen**	**hat gebacken**
to clean	**putzen**	**hat geputzt**
to clean up	**aufräumen**	**hat aufgeräumt**
to cook	**kochen**	**hat gekocht**
to mow	**mähen**	**hat gemäht**
to put	**stellen**	**hat gestellt**
to set	**setzen**	**hat gesetzt**
to sleep	**schlafen**	**hat geschlafen**
to watch TV	**fernsehen**	**hat ferngesehen**
to wash	**waschen**	**hat gewaschen**
to water	**gießen**	**hat gegossen**
in the yard	**im Garten**	
in the kitchen	**in der Küche**	
in the living room	**im Wohnzimmer**	
in the dining room	**im Esszimmer**	
in the bathroom	**im Bad**	
in the basement	**im Keller**	

Wo ist das? *Place an X in the column where you would most likely do each activity.*

	IM BAD (B)	IN DER KÜCHE (K)	IM WOHNZIMMER (W)
1. gießen	_____	_____	_____
2. backen	_____	_____	_____
3. kochen	_____	_____	_____
4. putzen	_____	_____	_____
5. waschen	_____	_____	_____
6. schlafen	_____	_____	_____
7. fernsehen	_____	_____	_____

Haben oder sein? *Place an X in the column that shows which helping verb is needed.*

	HABEN (H)	SEIN (S)
1. sein	_____	_____
2. haben	_____	_____
3. schwimmen	_____	_____
4. kaufen	_____	_____
5. fliegen	_____	_____
6. bleiben	_____	_____
7. machen	_____	_____
8. denken	_____	_____
9. laufen	_____	_____
10. anrufen	_____	_____
11. fahren	_____	_____
12. erzählen	_____	_____
13. wissen	_____	_____

Sätze schreiben (*Writing sentences*). *Rewrite the sentences in the conversational past/present perfect.*

1. Ilse bekommt den ersten Preis. _____

2. Meine Eltern kommen am Wochenende. _____

3. Wir haben keine Hausaufgaben. _____

4. Boris Becker spielt Tennis. _____

5. Ihr schlaft lange am Sonntag. _____

6. Frau Hennes, Sie wissen viel über Chemie. _____

7. Ich rufe meine Freundin an. _____

8. Wir fahren in die Berge. _____

9. Der Hans erzählt eine Geschichte. _____

10. Mein Lehrer fliegt nach Ägypten. _____

The simple past

29

Das Präteritum (*The simple past or written past*)

Also called the written past, the simple past tense functions just like the present perfect. The main difference from the present perfect is that the simple past is found in written texts and is rarely ever used in spoken language.

In English, *-ed* is placed at the end of the verb, as in:

walk   *walked*

Or sometimes the entire verb must change (*buy/bought*).

In German, as in English, it is the main verb that is conjugated in the simple past form.

to buy	kaufen	kaufte
to be	sein	war

Again, the verb form is differentiated based on the type of verb. This tense can mean that a person *was doing something*, *used to do something*, or *did something*.

Schwache Verben (*Weak verbs*)

The **er/sie/es** simple past forms of weak verbs usually look like the **er/sie/es** present tense form with an **-e** at the end:

fragen	fragte
machen	machte
spielen	spielte
manipulieren	manipulierte
studieren	studierte
erzählen	erzählte
verdienen	verdiente

ich -te	wir -ten
du -test	ihr -tet
er/sie/es -te	sie/Sie -ten

Ich kaufte ein Auto.	*I bought a car.*
Sie studierte Deutsch.	*She studied German.*

ÜBUNG 29·1

Change the following verb phrases to the past tense.

1. Ich lerne viel. _____

2. Frau Müller raucht. _____

3. Das Kind weint. _____

4. Atmest du? _____

5. Wir öffnen die Tür. _____

6. Die Jungen wohnen hier. _____

7. Arbeitet ihr? _____

8. Das Mädchen lächelt. _____

9. Ich wohne in Frankfurt. _____

10. Was sagst du? _____

ÜBUNG 29·2

Lücken ausfüllen. (*Fill in the blanks*.) *You and your friends are conversing about the past. Put the correct past tense form of the verb in each blank.*

1. (machen) Meine Eltern _____ viel mit uns.

2. (reisen) Wir _____ überall.

3. (machen) Ich _____ selten mit meiner Familie Urlaub.

4. (backen) Meine Oma _____ jeden Samstag Kuchen.

5. (kochen) Mein Vater _____ einmal die Woche für uns.

6. (schauen) Mein Bruder und ich _____ jeden Samstag Fernsehen.

7. (spielen) Alle Kinder _____ ein Instrument.

8. (mähen) _____ ihr auch einmal im Monat den Rasen?

9. (kaufen) Die Kusinen _____ immer CDs.

10. (putzen) Ich _____ jedes Wochenende das Bad.

Starke Verben (*Strong verbs*)

Strong verbs are not so easy. Sometimes they may seem to follow the the same pattern as similar English words.

sing	*sang*		singen	sang

Sometimes they may look completely different than the infinitive. They may even have a stem-vowel change.

be	*was*		sein	war

The easiest way to learn these is simply just to memorize each of these verbs. One thing is consistent for all of them—the set of endings for the different persons.

ich	-		wir	-en
du	-st		ihr	-t
er/sie/es	-		sie/Sie	-en

The stem is what changes every time. There are, however, some guidelines for the strong verbs. There are groupings in which a verb can fit, and sometimes it will follow a pattern. The grouping depends on the stem vowel of the infinitive, and these groupings also predict how the stem vowel will change in the simple past. Here are a few examples:

Group 1: e / ie to a

beginnen	began	*to begin*
finden	fand	*to find*
liegen	lag	*to lie*

Group 2: e / ie / ü to o

fliegen	flog	*to fly*
heben	hob	*to lift*
lügen	log	*to lie*

Group 3: ei to ie / i

beißen	biss	*to bite*
bleiben	blieb	*to stay*

Group 4: e / u / o to a

essen	aß	*to eat*
tun	tat	*to do*
kommen	kam	*to come*

Group 5: a to u

fahren	fuhr	*to drive*

ÜBUNG
29·3

Change the following present tense verbs to the past. Use the first- or third-person singular.

1. beißen _____

2. essen _____

3. finden _____

4. geben _____

5. gehen   _____

6. gewinnen   _____

7. heißen   _____

8. helfen   _____

9. kommen   _____

10. lügen   _____

11. sitzen   _____

12. sprechen   _____

13. tun   _____

Gemischte Verben (*Mixed verbs*)

Mixed verbs are a mix of weak (**-te**) and strong (stem-vowel change). There are relatively few of these. Because there are so few, they are all listed here:

brennen	brannte	*to burn*
bringen	brachte	*to bring*
denken	dachte	*to think*
kennen	kannte	*to know*
nennen	nannte	*to name*
rennen	rannte	*to run*
senden	sandte	*to send*
wenden	wandte	*to turn*
wissen	wusste	*to know*

Because of their similarity to the mixed verbs, modal auxiliary verbs change in a similar way. The umlaut is removed, and the weak verb ending is placed after the stem.

ÜBUNG
29·4

Change the following sentences to the simple past.

1. Oma bringt frische Petersilie aus ihrem Garten mit.

   _____

2. Er weiß, dass wir euch ein Päckchen senden.

   _____

3. Wir benennen das Baby.

   _____

4. Kennst du die Familie?

   _____

5. Bringen wir etwas mit zur Fete?

_____

6. Ich denke nach.

_____

7. Die Kinder rennen aus dem Haus.

_____

8. Sie wendet mir den Rücken.

_____

As always, there are some exceptions you need to make when forming the simple past. If a weak or mixed verb ends in -**d**, -**m**, -**n**, or -**t**, you must add an extra -**e** before adding the simple past ending -**te**.

arbeiten   arbeitete   *to work*

For certain verbs, the simple past is preferred to the conversational past. In other words, the simple past is used both in written and spoken German. These verbs are **haben**, **sein**, **werden**, and **wissen**.

haben	hatten	*to have*
sein	waren	*to be*
werden	wurden	*to become*
wissen	wussten	*to know*

Modal auxiliaries in the simple past

Modal auxiliaries in the simple past function much like the weak verbs. Take the stem of the infinitive and add the correct ending.

ich	-te		wir	-ten
du	-test		ihr	-tet
er/sie/es	-te		sie/Sie	-ten

This is the most frequent past tense form used for modals.

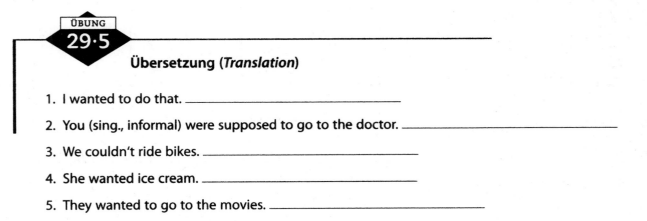

ÜBUNG
29·5

Übersetzung (*Translation*)

1. I wanted to do that. _____

2. You (sing., informal) were supposed to go to the doctor. _____

3. We couldn't ride bikes. _____

4. She wanted ice cream. _____

5. They wanted to go to the movies. _____

6. The boys weren't allowed to sleep long. _____

7. Maria was able to buy a new dress. _____

8. Were you (sing., informal) able to bring some cake? _____

Spaßfakten (*Fun facts*)

Idiomatische Ausdrücke (*Idiomatic expressions*)

At a restaurant or store

Was darf es sein?	May I help you? (store clerk)
Wenn ich bitten darf.	If you please.

At the doctor's office

Er kann Sie jetzt sprechen.	He can see you now. (doctor, dentist)

Out of frustration

Muss das sein? Is that really necessary?
So müsste es immer sein. That's how it should be all the time.
Das mag der Himmel verhüten! Heaven forbid!
Du sollst damit sofort aufhören! You're to stop that right now!
Was soll das (heißen)? What's that supposed to mean? What's the idea?
Es soll nicht wieder vorkommen. It won't happen again.
Sie könnten sich irren. You could be mistaken.
Das kann man wohl sagen. You can say that again.
Er kann Deutsch. He knows German. ("can German")
Ich muss nach Hause. I have to go home.
Das mag wohl sein. That well may be. / That may be so.
Er mag/mochte etwa 1,3 Meter groß sein. He must be/must have been about 1.3 meters tall.
Das Buch soll sehr gut sein. The book is said to be very good.
Das will nicht viel sagen. That's of little consequence. That doesn't mean much.
Er will es nicht gesehen haben. He claims not to have seen it.
Das hat er nicht gewollt. That's not what he intended.

The past perfect

30

Das Plusquamperfekt (*The past perfect*)

The past perfect (**das Plusquamperfekt**) clarifies actions that were completed or were being completed in the past, before something else that took place in the simple past or present perfect. In English we speak of what *had happened* before something else happened. It's the past past. For example:

> Before he went to the university, he had graduated from high school with honors.
> Because she had been studying for hours on Sunday night, she was very tired in school yesterday.

This past tense looks almost identical to the present perfect. Only the helping verbs **haben** and **sein** are different. To make this tense, you need to change **haben** and **sein** to their simple past forms: **hatten** and **waren**. Conjugate them in their correct form, according to the subject, and put the participle at the end of the sentence.

ich	hatte	war	wir	hatten	waren
du	hattest	warst	ihr	hattet	wart
er/sie/es	hatte	war	sie/Sie	hatten	waren

> Bevor er an die Uni ging, hatte er seinen Abschluss an dem High School gemacht.
> Weil sie Sonntagabend viele Stunden gelernt hatte, war sie gestern in der Schule sehr müde.

What does make the use of this tense somewhat difficult is the mandatory addition of a conjunction (a word that joins two sentences together). These will be more closely examined in Chapters 43 and 44. For now, we will confine ourselves to the conjunctions **weil** (*because*), **bevor** (*before*), and **nachdem** (*after*).

ÜBUNG
30·1

Hatte oder war? *Write the correct auxiliary verb in each blank.*

1. Wir _____ nach Griechenland geflogen.

2. Ich _____ meine Hausaufgabe nicht gemacht.

3. Meine Eltern _____ das Haus gebaut.

4. Der Regensturm _____ zu schnell gekommen.

5. Die Lehrerin _____ krank gewesen.

6. _____ ihr am Markt eingekauft?

7. Die anderen Schüler _____ am Montag keinen Unterricht gehabt.

8. Ich _____ ein Geschenk für Sabine mitgebracht.

9. Heiko _____ mit dem Auto gefahren.

10. In der Kirche _____ wir ein schönes Lied gesungen.

Bis sie verletzt wurde ... (Until she got hurt . . .) *What could Marika do until she got hurt?*

1. (sie spielt jeden Tag Fußball): Bis sie verletzt wurde, _____

2. (sie schwimmt im Schwimmbad): Bis sie verletzt wurde, _____

3. (sie fliegt in den Urlaub zum Bergsteigen): Bis sie verletzt wurde, _____

4. (sie läuft einen Marathon): Bis sie verletzt wurde, _____

5. (sie trägt alles in den dritten Stockwerk): Bis sie verletzt wurde, _____

6. (sie sieht mit Freunden einen Film im Kino): Bis sie verletzt wurde, _____

7. (sie geht oft nach der Schule ins Kino): Bis sie verletzt wurde, _____

8. (sie besucht ihre Großeltern): Bis sie verletzt wurde, _____

9. (sie saugt in der ganzen Wohnung Staub): Bis sie verletzt wurde, _____

10. (sie tanzt in der Disko): Bis sie verletzt wurde, _____

·VII·

Grammar

Vocabulary

Fun facts

The future tense
Future time expressions

31

Das Futur (*The future tense*)

The verb **werden** usually denotes the future tense (**das Futur**)—an action that takes place sometime in the future.

Werden

ich werde	*I am going to*	wir werden	*we are going to*
du wirst	*you (sing., informal) are going to*	ihr werdet	*you (pl., informal) are going to*
er/sie/es wird	*he/she/it is going to*	sie/Sie werden	*they/you (formal) are going to*

Werden sends the meaning-carrying verb that it accompanies to the end of the sentence in the infinitive form, as demonstrated in this example sentence:

> Ich werde morgen nach der Schule ab 16 Uhr mit meinen Freunden ins Kino gehen.
> *I am going to go to the movies with my friends tomorrow after school, sometime after 4.*

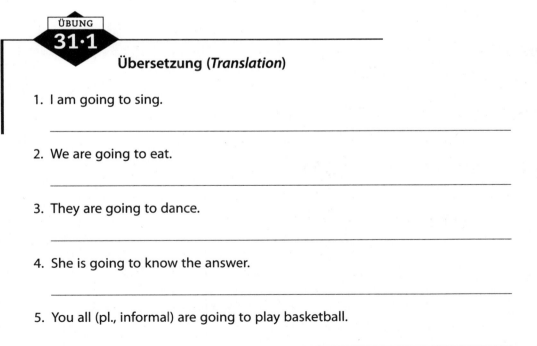

ÜBUNG
31·1

Übersetzung (*Translation*)

1. I am going to sing.

   _____

2. We are going to eat.

   _____

3. They are going to dance.

   _____

4. She is going to know the answer.

   _____

5. You all (pl., informal) are going to play basketball.

   _____

6. Mr. Schulz, are you going to go to the movies?

_____

7. What are we going to do tomorrow?

_____

8. I'm not going to do anything.

_____

9. You (sing., informal) are going to do your homework.

_____

10. They're going to live in Germany.

_____

WORTSCHATZ

Future time expressions

later	**später**	this morning	**heute Morgen**
next month	**nächsten Monat**	tomorrow	**morgen**
next week	**nächste Woche**	tomorrow afternoon	**morgen Nachmittag**
next year	**nächstes Jahr**	tomorrow morning	**morgen früh**
the day after tomorrow	**übermorgen**	tomorrow night	**morgen Abend**
this afternoon	**heute Nachmittag**	tonight	**heute Nacht**
this evening	**heute Abend**		

ÜBUNG
31·2

Übersetzung (*Translation*)

1. I'm going to bed at 10 tonight.

_____

2. He's going to brush his teeth tomorrow morning.

_____

3. Are you (sing., informal) going to take a bath later?

_____

4. Next week we are going to get married.

_____

5. They are going to buy a car next month.

_____

6. You all (pl., informal) will have a test the day after tomorrow.

_____

7. You all (pl., informal) are going to eat tonight.

_____

The future perfect

32

Das Futur II (*The future perfect tense*)

The future perfect tense (**das Futur II**) is used to talk about something we will have done by a specific time in the future. It is somewhat rare in German.

> Bis Dezember werde ich alle
> Geschenke gekauft haben.
> *By December I will have bought
> all the presents.*

To form this tense, **werden** not only sends the meaning-carrying verb to the end of the sentence (in the form of the past participle), but also sends the helping or auxiliary verb (**haben** or **sein**, in the infinitive) to the end of the sentence as well, in the final position after the past participle.

ÜBUNG
32·1
Übersetzung (*Translation*)

1. By nine o'clock I will have played tennis for three hours.

   _____

2. She will have danced all night.

   _____

3. They will have been sitting here for two hours.

   _____

4. We will have bought the house by next year.

   _____

5. Before he turns 21 he will have gone to Europe.

   _____

6. You (pl., informal) all will have done the homework by tomorrow.

   _____

7. They will have gone shopping by Monday.

   _____

The passive
Chores
Adverbs of time

33

Das Passiv (*The passive*)

The passive (**das Passiv**) is rare and/or discouraged in English due to its imprecision. In fact, it's usually only used when the agent or actor in the sentence needs to remain unnamed. Take this example:

> *The window was broken last night.*

We don't know who broke the window, but we know that someone or something broke it. It is no longer in one piece. The emphasis is on the recipient of the action. In this example, the writer wants to emphasize that the *window* is broken, regardless of who or what broke it.

The passive is a very common tense in German, and it is frequently found in written texts.

> Der Ball wird geschlagen. *The ball is hit.*

You form the passive in German by using a form of the verb **werden** along with the past participle. It looks deceptively similar to the past tense. It's no different in English.

> *The team was defeated 100 to 99.*

The subject of a passive sentence is actually the direct object of the active sentence. It determines the form of **werden** (which can only take one of two forms in the passive, the third person singular or plural). The grammatical subject of the passive sentence experiences the action; it doesn't perform the action.

WORTSCHATZ

Zu Hause helfen (*Chores*)

das Bett machen	to make the bed	**den Müll sortieren**	to sort the trash (recycle)
die Blumen gießen	to water the flowers	**den Rasen mähen**	to mow the lawn
die Fenster putzen	to wash/clean the windows	**den Tisch abräumen**	to clear the table
das Geschirr spülen	to wash the dishes	**den Tisch decken**	to set the table
den Hund füttern	to feed the dog	**das Zimmer aufräumen**	to pick up the room

---

Zeitadverbien (Adverbs of time)

alle …	every …	**selten**	seldom
einmal im / in der …	once every …	**jeden Abend**	every night
immer	always	**jeden Tag**	every day
meistens	usually	**jeden Morgen**	every morning
nie	never	**am Wochenende**	on the weekend
oft	often		

ÜBUNG
33·1

Lücken ausfüllen. (Fill in the blanks.) *Fill in each blank with the correct form of* **werden** *and the past participle.*

1. Die Hausaufgaben _____ jeden Abend _____.

2. Der Hund _____ zweimal am Tag _____.

3. Der Müll _____ einmal pro Woche _____.

4. Die Blumen _____ alle zwei Wochen _____.

5. Die Betten _____ jeden Morgen _____.

6. Das Geschirr _____ nie _____.

7. Der Rasen _____ einmal im Monat _____.

8. Der Tisch _____ nur am Wochenende _____.

9. Nach dem Essen _____ der Tisch immer _____.

10. Das Zimmer von meinem Bruder _____ selten _____.

Using the passive in different tenses

The passive can be used in the future, present, and past tenses. Because the verb **werden** is the conjugated verb, its tense indicates the time frame of the sentence.

Der Ball wird geschlagen.	*The ball is being hit.*
Der Ball wird geschlagen werden.	*The ball will be hit.*
Der Ball wurde geschlagen.	*The ball was hit.*
Der Ball ist geschlagen geworden.	*The ball has been hit.*

Übersetzung (*Translation*)

1. The song was sung. _____

2. The book is written. _____

3. The glass has been broken. _____

4. The food has been eaten. _____

5. The chairs were taken. _____

6. The room will have been cleaned. _____

7. The newspapers are being read. _____

8. The children are being taught. _____

9. German was studied. _____

10. The games were played. _____

Subjunctive II

34

Der Konjunktiv II (*The subjunctive II or conditional*)

No, putting the subjunctive II (**der Konjunktiv II**) before the subjunctive I (Chapter 35) was not an editorial error! The subjunctive II is the more common of the two, and the subjunctive I can only be found when you read or watch anything news related. (The subjunctive I is called indirect speech, and it removes any responsibility from the speaker or writer if another person is misquoted.) The subjunctive II is used when referring to wishes, conditional situations, and polite requests.

> *If I had a million dollars, I would . . .*
> *If I could be any animal I wanted, I would be . . .*
> *I would be happy if I could sleep in tomorrow.*

Formation of the conditional

Both subjunctive moods are based, like the passive, on the past tense. Here we take the simple past of **haben** (**hatten**) and **sein** (**waren**) and put an umlaut over the stem **a**.

Wenn ich eine Million Dollar hätte, wäre ich reich.	*If I had a million dollars, I would be rich.*
Wenn ich nur jünger wäre!	*If only I were younger!*

As you can see, the conjunction **wenn** is used to introduce the conditional. Sometimes it can be omitted.

Ich wäre reich, hätte ich eine Million Dollar.	*I would be rich, if I had a million dollars.*

Another common form of the conditional is the **würden** (**werden**/*to become*) + infinitive construction.

ich würde	wir würden
du würdest	ihr würdet
er/sie/es würde	sie/Sie würden

The main verb, carrying the meaning, then goes to the end of the sentence in its infinitive form.

Lücken ausfüllen. (*Fill in the blanks.*) *Fill in each blank with the correct form of either* **haben** *or* **sein.**

1. _____ ich genug Geld, würde ich nicht arbeiten.

2. _____ ich größer, würde ich nicht nach Hilfe fragen.

3. _____ mein Vater eine Frau, wäre er meine Mutter.

4. _____ wir ein eigenes Haus, würden wir nicht in einer Wohnung wohnen.

5. _____ er nicht in der Schule, würde er in ein Café gehen.

6. _____ er keine Hausaufgaben, würde er Freizeit haben.

7. _____ ihr meine Freunde nicht, wäre ich sehr traurig.

Wenn ich nur!!! *Fill in the blanks with the correct form of* **würden.**

1. Wenn er nur anrufen _____!

2. Wenn wir bloß wissen _____!

3. Wenn Sie uns keine Hausaufgaben geben _____!

4. Wenn ihr nur umziehen _____!

5. Wenn ich nur schlafen _____!

6. Wenn wir das Haus aufräumen _____!

WORTSCHATZ

Adjectives describing states of being

arm	poor	**reich**	rich
gestresst	stressed	**entspannt**	relaxed
krank	ill	**gesund**	healthy
müde	tired	**wach**	awake
schlecht	bad	**gut**	well

The subjunctive can also be formed by any verb. Just conjugate the verb in the simple past and add an umlaut to the vowel in the stem if it is **a**, **o**, or **u**. The most common verbs used in the subjunctive are the modal verbs and the verb **werden**, but any verbs will work.

ÜBUNG
34·3

Lücken ausfüllen. (Fill in the blanks.) *Fill in each blank with the correct form of the verb given.*

1. (können) _____ ich ein Flugzeug fliegen, würde ich sofort nach Ägypten.

2. (dürfen) _____ ich Auto fahren, würde ich nach Kanada fahren.

3. (spielen) _____ ich Tennis, würde ich gegen Serena Williams spielen.

4. (wollen) _____ ich eine Pause machen, würde ich schlafen.

5. (haben) _____ ich Energie, würde ich ins Fitnesszentrum gehen.

6. (mögen) _____ ich ein Eis, würde ich Zitroneneis essen.

7. (wollen) _____ ich Geld verspielen, würde ich nach Las Vegas gehen.

Spaßfakten (*Fun facts*)

"Mein Hut"

"**Mein Hut**" is a very famous children's song in German, and half of the song is in the subjunctive form.

> *Mein Hut, der hat drei Ecken,*
> *Drei Ecken hat mein Hut,*
> *Und hätt' er nicht drei Ecken,*
> *dann wär' er nicht mein Hut.*

Subjunctive I

35

Der Konjunktiv I (*The subjunctive I*)

The subjunctive I (**der Konjunktiv I**) is not used as much as the subjunctive II, as it is extremely formal. You will find its form in written texts when someone other than the writer is being quoted (indirect speech). Because it is only found in this specialized context, it is more important for you to be able to recognize it when you see it than it is for you to produce it yourself.

The third person is the most common form of the subjunctive I. To form this mood, take the stem and add the subjunctive I endings. Verbs are formed by taking the stem and adding the following endings (same as subjunctive II):

ich -e	wir -en
du -est	ihr -et
er/sie/es -e	sie/Sie -en

ich habe	wir haben
du habest	ihr habet
er/sie/es habe	sie/Sie haben

Because the subjunctive I is formed from the stem of the infinitive, the conjugation of **sein** in this tense looks quite different from the other tenses of this verb.

ich sei	wir seien
du seist	ihr seiet
er/sie/es sei	sie/Sie seien

ÜBUNG
35·1

Nachrichten schreiben. *Rewrite the following sentences, putting the second verb in each statement in the subjunctive I.*

1. Er sagt, er sagt es nicht.

_____

2. Sie sagt, sie hat es nicht.

_____

3. Sie sagen, sie haben es nicht getan.

_____

143

4. Sie sagt, sie ist nicht zu Hause.

_____

5. Er sagt, er hat nichts gehört.

_____

6. Sie sagen, sie wissen nicht, was passiert ist.

_____

7. Sie sagt, das Land soll keinen Krieg führen.

_____

8. Er sagt, der Autohersteller ist in diesem Fall schuldig.

_____

9. Sie sagen, sie lebt schon seit 10 Jahren in der Stadt.

_____

10. Sie sagen, der Schüler kann kein Türkisch sprechen.

_____

Spaßfakten (*Fun facts*)

Deutsches Fernsehen (*German television*)

In Germany there is one major central station that can be received by every television, whether or not it is hooked up to cable: ARD (**Allgemeiner Rundfunk Deutschlands** or **Arbeitsgemeinschaft der öffentlich-rechtlichen Rundfunkanstalten der Bundesrepublik Deutschland**—"*Consortium of public-law broadcasting institutions of the Federal Republic of Germany*"). Founded shortly after the Second World War in West Germany, its purpose was to be a joint venture of public broadcasting. Its nickname is **Das Erste**.

    Each region also receives a free public station. The most famous are NDR (**Norddeutscher Rundfunk**), WDR (**Westdeutscher Rundfunk**), SWR (**Südwestrundfunk**), BR (**Bayerischer Rundfunk**), and MDR (**Mitteldeutscher Rundfunk**).

·VIII·

Adverbs
Interrogative pronouns

·36·

Das Adverb (*Adverbs*)

Adverbs modify not only the verb, or action word, in the sentence, but they can also describe another adverb or adjective. Their purpose is to answer questions such as *how, why, when,* and *to what extent.* English adverbs end in *-ly*; German adverbs sometimes end in **-lich**, but there are many other adverbs as well that take different forms.

WORTSCHATZ

Adverbien

Zeit (*Time*)

abends (am Abend)	in the evening	**morgen**	tomorrow
bald	soon	**morgens (am Morgen)**	in the morning
damals	at that time	**nachmittags**	in the afternoon
dann	then	**(am Nachmittag)**	in the afternoon
erst	not until	**nachts (in der Nacht)**	at night
früh	early	**nie/nimmer**	never
gestern	yesterday	**noch**	still
gleich/sofort	immediately	**oft**	often
heute	today	**schon**	already
immer	always	**selten**	seldom
jetzt/nun	now	**spät(er)**	late(r)
manchmal	sometimes	**täglich**	daily

Weise (*Manner*)

außerordentlich	extremely	**leicht**	easily
deutlich	clearly	**leider**	sadly
endlich	finally	**natürlich**	naturally
fröhlich/gern	happily	**offentsichtlich**	obviously
gänzlich	perfectly	**wahrscheinlich**	probably
gewöhnlich	usually	**wirklich**	absolutely
häufig	frequently	**schnell**	fast/rapidly
langsam	slowly	**selten**	rarely

147

Ort (Place)

da/dort	there	**nahe**	near
draußen	outside	**nirgends**	nowhere
drinnen	inside	**oben**	above
drüben	over there	**rechts**	right
fern	distant	**überall**	everywhere
hier	here	**unten**	below
hinten	back there	**weg**	away
irgendwo	somewhere	**weit**	far/widely
links	left	**zurück**	back

Wortfolge (Word order)

Generally, adverbs appear as close to the verb as possible. This means that they will normally take the first or third position in a sentence.

ÜBUNG
36·1

Was können sie gut machen? (*What can these persons do well?*) *Explain what each person does well using* **gut.**

1. Magic Johnson und Michael Jordan (basketball) _____

2. Maria Sharapova (tennis) _____

3. Edgar Allan Poe (write) _____

4. Plácido Domingo (sing) _____

5. Céline Dion (sing) _____

6. Richard Petty (drive) _____

7. Ronaldo (soccer) _____

ÜBUNG
36·2

A, B, oder C?

1. _____ Junge Leute gehen _____ ins Kino.

     a. nie   b. oft   c. gestern

2. _____ Ich soll _____ Wasser trinken.

     a. selten   b. immer   c. morgen

3. _____ Normalerweise schlafen Menschen _____.

    a. draußen   b. nirgends   c. drinnen

4. _____ Der Weihnachtsmann besucht ein Haus _____.

    a. selten   b. bald   c. später

5. _____ Man muss _____ atmen.

    a. immer   b. nimmer   c. selten

6. _____ Der Garten ist am Haus _____.

    a. ständig   b. hinten   c. schnell

7. _____ Ein Hase läuft _____.

    a. schnell   b. langsam   c. wahrscheinlich

ÜBUNG
36·3

Wo ist das? (*Where is that?*)

1. ein Baum _____

2. eine Lampe _____

3. der Mond _____

4. ich _____

5. der Rücken _____

6. Sauerstoff (*oxygen*) _____

7. die rechte Hand _____

Das Fragepronomen (*The interrogative pronoun*)

The interrogative pronoun begins an interrogative question or statement. In other words, it introduces a question or statement that seeks information and/or an answer. It can refer either to a person (*who?*) or to abstract concepts (*what? when? where? why?* etc.).

wer?	*who*	wie?	*how*
wen?	*who(m)* (acc.)	wie viel?	*how much*
wem?	*(to) who(m)* (dat.)	wo?	*where*
wessen?	*whose*	wohin?	*where to*
was?	*what*	woher?	*where from*

Übersetzung (_Translation_)

1. Why weren't you (sing., informal) at the party?

   _____

2. What does she see?

   _____

3. Where will we go after school?

   _____

4. Who should answer the question?

   _____

5. Why can't we go?

   _____

6. What is he doing?

   _____

7. When can we eat?

   _____

8. (To) whom is he giving the ring?

   _____

9. Whose shoes are those?

   _____

10. How much does the dog cost?

   _____

ÜBUNG

36·5

Was war die Frage? (_What was the question?_) _Create a question for each answer._

1. Sie hat **ein Kleid** getragen.

   _____

2. Er hat **eine ganze Pizza** gegessen.

   _____

3. Wir haben **die Sängerin** gehört.

_____

4. Das Auto hat **nur €1.000** gekostet.

_____

5. Wir können nicht gehen, **denn wir müssen noch die Hausaufgaben machen.**

_____

6. Sie gehen **um 20 Uhr** ins Kino.

_____

7. **Meine Eltern** fahren nach Mexiko.

_____

8. Die Schildkröte läuft **langsam**.

_____

Prepositions—accusative

37

Akkusativpräpositionen
(Accusative prepositions)

Prepositions (**die Präpositionen**) are meant to show the relationship between two nouns or other sentence structures when relating to time, manner, place, or direction. These prepositions also demand cases for their objects.

The prepositions listed below rule the accusative case, which means that the object of the preposition must be in the accusative case. Fortunately this means that, compared to the base, or nominative, case, only the masculine object is affected—for the two other genders and for the plural, the forms stay the same from nominative to accusative.

NOMINATIVE	ACCUSATIVE
der Mann	den Mann
ein Mann	einen Mann
er	ihn

Die Akkusativpräpositionen

bis	*until*
durch	*through*
entlang	*along*
für	*for*
gegen	*against*
um	*around, about, at; at (time)*

	NOMINATIVE	ACCUSATIVE
Masculine	der Mann	den Mann
Feminine	die Frau	die Frau
Neuter	das Kind	das Kind
Plural	die Kinder	die Kinder

Wir haben etwas für unseren Vater.	*We have something for our father.*
Die Schule spielt gegen eine gute Mannschaft.	*The school is playing against a good team.*
Die Kinder laufen um das Haus.	*The children run around the house.*
Die Schüler gehen durch die Gänge.	*The students go through the halls.*

Hinweis (*Note*): Normally, a prepositional phrase consists of the preposition followed by the noun; with **entlang**, however, the word order changes. When you use **entlang**, the noun is followed by the preposition.

　　　　　Wir spazieren den Fluss entlang.　　　　　*We walk along the river.*

ÜBUNG
37·1

Lücken ausfüllen. (*Fill in the blanks.*) *Choose the correct preposition (**für**, **bis**, **um**) to fill in each blank.*

1. Hier geht es _____ das Prinzip.

2. Das Haus haben sie _____ uns gekauft.

3. Ich arbeite _____ fünfzehn Uhr.

4. Meine Freundin hat _____ 30 Euro zwei Pullover gekauft.

5. Die Katze läuft _____ den Stuhl.

6. Wir können _____ dich den Rasen mähen.

7. Dankst du dem Opa _____ das schöne Geschenk?

8. Gehen wir _____ 20 Uhr?

ÜBUNG
37·2

Lücken ausfüllen. (*Fill in the blanks*). *Using the cues provided, fill in each blank with the appropriate object.*

1. (du) Ich kann für _____ das Geschirr spülen.

2. (wer) Gegen _____ spielen wir heute nach der Schule?

3. (die Frau) Der Ring ist für _____.

4. (er) Kommst du ohne _____?

5. (das Haus) Die Kinder laufen durch _____.

6. (der Fluss) Der Junge und das Mädchen gehen _____ entlang.

7. (sein Sohn) Er kauft das Spielzeug für _____.

8. (dein) Darf ich dich um _____ Namen bitten?

9. (ihre Tante) Warum sagst du etwas gegen _____?

10. (der Saal) Der Vogel ist durch _____ geflogen.

Übersetzung (*Translation*)

1. The party begins at eight o'clock. _____

2. The presents are for you (sing., informal). _____

3. The girls walked along the river. _____

4. I never leave the house without a book. _____

5. Our school plays against a bad team tomorrow. _____

6. We must run through the rain. _____

7. The bird flew against the window. _____

8. The people vote for the president. _____

9. She is mowing the lawn for her parents. _____

10. He is working until five o'clock P.M. _____

Prepositions—dative

38

Dativpräpositionen (*Dative prepositions*)

Just like for the accusative case, there are some prepositions that rule the dative case.

Die Dativpräpositionen

aus	*out, from*
außer	*except*
bei, beim	*at, by*
gegenüber	*across from*
mit	*with*
nach	*after*
seit	*since*
von, vom	*from, of, by*
zu, zum, zur	*to, for*

Hinweis (*Note*): With **gegenüber** there is again a change in word order (as with **entlang** for the accusative prepositions). **Gegenüber** follows its object.

Ich sitze einem Mann gegenüber.	*I am sitting across from a man.*

	NOMINATIVE	ACCUSATIVE	DATIVE
Masculine	der Mann	den Mann	dem Mann
Feminine	die Frau	die Frau	der Frau
Neuter	das Kind	das Kind	dem Kind
Plural	die Kinder	die Kinder	den Kindern

Hinweis (*Note*): In the dative, all of the articles look like versions of the (nominative) masculine articles. But do not be misled or confused by this; the genders are as shown in the chart above.

Hinweis (*Note*): Whenever possible, add an **-n** to the end of a dative plural object.

Dativpronomen und Possessivpronomen
(*Dative pronouns and possessive pronouns*)

mir	*me*	uns	*you (pl.)*
dir	*you (sing.)*	euch	*them*
ihm	*him*	ihnen	*you*
ihr	*her*	Ihnen	*you (formal)*
ihm	*us*		

	MASCULINE	FEMININE	NEUTER	PLURAL
my	meinem	meiner	meinem	meinen
your (sing.)	deinem	deiner	deinem	deinen
his/its	seinem	seiner	seinem	seinen
her	ihrem	ihrer	ihrem	ihren
our	unsrem	unsrer	unsrem	unsren
your (pl.)	eurem	eurer	eurem	euren
their	ihrem	ihrer	ihrem	ihren
your (formal)	Ihrem	Ihrer	Ihrem	Ihren

ÜBUNG 38·1

Lücken ausfüllen. (*Fill in the blanks*.) *Choose the correct preposition to fill in each blank.*

1. Ich wohne noch _____ meinen Eltern.

2. _____ wem gehst du zum Ball?

3. Wir sitzen deinen Eltern _____ .

4. Sie arbeitet hier _____ 20 Jahren.

5. Mein Vater muss noch _____ der Post.

6. Alle gehen ins Schwimmbad _____ den Jungen.

7. Kommst du endlich mal _____ dem Bad?

8. Meine Freunde spielen Fußball _____ der Schule.

ÜBUNG 38·2

Lücken ausfüllen. (*Fill in the blanks*.) *Using the cues provided, fill in the blank with the appropriate object.*

1. (das Sofa) Die Lampe steht _____ gegenüber.

2. (wer) Mit _____ gehst du ins Kino?

3. (ich) Das Geschenk ist von _____ .

4. (die Schüler) Wir fahren mit _____ .

5. (das Haus) Mein Sohn läuft aus _____ .

6. (die Lehrer) Alle gehen nach Hause außer_____ .

7. (du) Ich fahre mit dem Auto zu _____ .

8. (dein) Können wir zu _____ Großeltern gehen?

9. (der Abend) Wir sind nach _____ so müde.

10. (ihre Freunde) Meine Eltern essen bei _____.

Übersetzung (*Translation*)

1. I go to the university. _____

2. Will you see a movie with me? _____

3. Since yesterday I have had a headache. _____

4. The presents are from us. _____

5. We are standing across from him. _____

6. All children except them are drinking milk. _____

7. The boys are coming out of the school. _____

Prepositions—genitive Geography

39

Genitivpräpositionen (*Genitive prepositions*)

The two main functions of the genitive prepositions are to show (1) the relationship between two nouns or (2) a possession. Most of the prepositions will include the word *of* when translated into English.

The genitive is a curious case. It is frequently misused or ignored by native German speakers. Some people say that in order to sound more truly "German" you should use the dative case instead of the genitive. In some cases, there is no choice but to use the dative form of the pronoun after a genitive preposition.

wegen ihr	*because of her*
trotz ihm	*despite him*

Here you will see the genitive in its pure form:

Die Genitivpräpositionen

(an)statt	*instead of*
außerhalb	*outside of*
diesseits	*this side of*
innerhalb	*inside of*
jenseits	*that side of*
laut	*according to*
oberhalb	*above*
trotz	*despite*
unterhalb	*underneath*
während	*during*
wegen	*because of*

WORTSCHATZ

Geografie (*Geography*)

der Berg	mountain	**die See**	sea
das Dorf	village	**der See**	lake
der Fluss	river	**der Staat**	state
die Innenstadt	downtown	**die Stadt**	city
das Land	country	**das Tal**	valley
das Meer	ocean	**wohnen**	to live

Lücken ausfüllen. (Fill in the blanks.) *Fill in each blank with the correct preposition.*

(outside of)   1. Wir wohnen _____ der Innenstadt.

(that side of)   2. Er wohnt _____ des Flusses.

(this side of)   3. Wohnst du _____ des Berges?

(above)   4. Sie wohnen _____ des Tales.

(inside of)   5. Ihr wohnt _____ der Stadt.

(despite)   6. Wir gehen _____ des Schnees.

(because of)   7. Sie fährt nicht _____ des Wetters.

Lücken ausfüllen. (Fill in the blanks.) *Fill in the blank with the correct form of each noun phrase.*

(der Mann)   1. Laut _____ sollen wir nicht im Regen fahren.

(die Stunde)   2. Während _____ gibt es keine Pause.

(das Mädchen)   3. Anstatt _____ kam der Assistent.

(die Schule)   4. Wegen _____ muss ich viel lernen.

(die See)   5. Jenseits _____ ist ein anderes Land.

(das Haus)   6. Außerhalb _____ liegt der Garten.

(das Dorf)   7. Innerhalb _____ wohnen die Bürger.

(der Saft)   8. Statt _____ tranken wir Milch.

Prepositions—accusative/dative Furniture

40

Wechselpräpositionen (Two-way prepositions)

Accusative/dative, or two-way, prepositions fluctuate depending on the verb. If the verb shows an action (**wohin?**), the preposition rules the accusative case. If the verb denotes a location (**wo?**), the preposition rules the dative case.

Ich stelle die Lampe in die Ecke.	*I set the lamp in the corner.*
Die Lampe steht in der Ecke.	*The lamp stands in the corner.*

Usually, when the preposition is accusative, a living item is acting as the agent in the sentence.

Die Wechselpräpositionen

an	*against*	über	*over*
auf	*on top of*	unter	*under*
hinter	*behind*	vor	*in front of*
in	*in*	zwischen	*between*
neben	*next to*		

Two-way verbs

stellen	*to set vertically*	stehen	*to stand*
setzen	*to set*	sitzen	*to sit*
legen	*to lay*	liegen	*to lie*
hängen	*to hang*		

WORTSCHATZ

Die Möbel (*Furniture*)

der Backofen	oven	**der Schreibtisch**	desk
das Bett	bed	**der Sessel**	armchair
das Bücherregal	bookshelf	**das Sofa**	sofa, couch
der Fernseher	television	**die Spülmaschine**	dishwasher
der Herd	range	**die Stehlampe**	floor lamp
die Kommode	chest of drawers	**der Stuhl**	chair
der Kühlschrank	refrigerator	**das Telefon**	telephone
die Lampe	lamp	**der Trockner**	dryer
der Nachttisch	nightstand	**die Waschmaschine**	washer
das Poster	poster		

ÜBUNG 40·1

Wo steht das? *Mark the appropriate location:* **in der Küche** *(K) or* **im Schlafzimmer** *(S).*

	K	S
1. der Herd	_____	_____
2. das Bett	_____	_____
3. die Kommode	_____	_____
4. der Kühlschrank	_____	_____
5. der Nachttisch	_____	_____
6. die Spülmaschine	_____	_____
7. der Backofen	_____	_____
8. die Waschmaschine	_____	_____

ÜBUNG 40·2

Übersetzung (*Translation*)

1. I have a washer. _____

2. We have two nightstands. _____

3. There are three rooms. _____

4. They have a dishwasher. _____

5. There are two armchairs in the living room. _____

6. There is a telephone in the kitchen. _____

7. Do you (sing., informal) have a refrigerator? _____

8. He doesn't have a dryer. _____

Wohin und wo? *First, state where you are putting the item (accusative); then, describe where it is (dative).*

1. ich / stellen / die Lampe / auf / der Tisch

   _____

2. die Lampe / stehen / auf / der Tisch

   _____

3. ich / setzen / die Katze / unter / der Stuhl

   _____

4. die Katze / sitzen / unter / der Stuhl

   _____

5. ich / legen / die Zeitung / auf / die Couch

   _____

6. die Zeitung / liegen / auf / die Couch

   _____

7. ich / hängen / das Poster / an / die Wand / über / das Bett

   _____

8. das Poster / hängen / an / die Wand / über / das Bett

   _____

Lücken ausfüllen. (*Fill in the blanks.*) *Choose the correct preposition to put in each blank.*

1. an / auf / in   Wir hängen das Bild _____ die Wand.

2. vor / neben / zwischen   Die Katze steht _____ den zwei Bäumen.

3. in / vor / zwischen   Der Baum steht _____ dem Haus.

4. an / in / hinter   Meine Mutti legt meine Klamotten _____ meine Kommode.

5. vor / auf / an   Papa stellt die Leiter _____ das Haus.

6. über / unter / in   Die Hängelampe hängt _____ dem Teppich.

7. über / unter / neben   Der Teppich liegt _____ dem Bett.

8. an / in / vor   Die Familie sitzt _____ dem Tisch und isst.

9. neben / zwischen / in   Mein bester Freund steht _____ mir links.

10. an / auf / in   Der Vogel landet _____ das Haus.

Spaßfakten (*Fun facts*)

Der Garten

Germans love bringing the green outdoors to their living space.

- A park is called a **Garten**. Famous **Gärten** in Germany are the Berlin **Tiergarten** and the **Englischer Garten** in München.
- A front yard is called a **Vorgarten**, and a backyard is called a **Hintergarten**.
- Even people who live in city apartments sometimes have a garden (**Schrebergarten**). These are small plots in large groupings that can be found on the outskirts of towns and are rented. On the weekend they are usually full of overnighters trying to escape the noise and bustle of the city.

Grammar

Vocabulary

Fun facts

Da- and **wo**- compounds ◆·41·◆

Komposita mit da- und wo-
(Da- *and* **wo**- *compounds*)

Compounds with **da**- and **wo**- serve one main purpose: to shorten a sentence when the object of the prepositional phrase has been mentioned in a previous statement.

Steht die Lampe auf dem Nachttisch?	*Is the lamp on the nightstand?*
Ja, sie steht darauf.	*Yes, it's there.*

Wo- compounds are used in questions; **da**- compounds are used in statements. However, these compounds can only be used when referring to an inanimate object. You must use a prepositional phrase when referring to a person.

If a preposition begins with a vowel, you must first insert an -**r**- before writing the preposition.

da + neben = daneben
da + an = daran

ÜBUNG
41·1

Antwort zur Frage. *Create a question from each statement by inserting the correct* **wo**- *compound or, if a* **wo**- *compound cannot be used, the correct prepositional phrase.*

1. Ich spiele morgen mit Sabine Tennis. _____ spielst du Tennis?

2. Wir fahren mit dem Zug nach Berlin. _____ fahrt ihr?

3. Er hat Angst vor Spinnen. _____ hat er Angst?

4. Wir sprechen über Kunst. _____ sprecht ihr?

5. Sie spricht über ihren Freund. _____ spricht sie?

6. Die Zeitung ist auf dem Tisch. _____ ist die Zeitung?

7. Ich glaube an dich. _____ glaubst du?

8. Der Hund ist unter dem Stuhl. _____ ist der Hund?

*Respond to the following questions by saying yes and using a **da-** compound or, if a **da-** compound cannot be used, the correct prepositional phrase.*

1. Bist du gegen den Krieg? _____

2. Bist du für Frieden? _____

3. Denkst du an die Schule? _____

4. Sitzt die Katze auf der Couch? _____

5. Gehst du ins Café? _____

6. Hast du schon über das Buch gesprochen? _____

7. Liegt der Hund unter dem Bett? _____

8. Stehst du neben dem Baum? _____

9. Stehst du neben der Lehrerin? _____

10. Gehst du ins Kino? _____

Create a question you would ask to get the answer provided.

1. Er sitzt auf der Bank. _____

2. Sie hat das Bild an die Wand gehängt. _____

3. Wir fliegen mit einem 747 nach Istanbul. _____

4. Ich glaube an mich selbst. _____

5. Das Mädchen hat das Kleid von ihrer Oma bekommen. _____

6. Der Lehrer fragt nach der Hausaufgabe. _____

7. Die Tiere kommen aus dem Zoo. _____

8. Das dient zu guter Leistung. _____

9. Die Katze sitzt in der Badewanne. _____

10. Wir fahren nach Kanada. _____

Word order—statements and questions

·42·

For the most part, German and English word order (**die Wortstellung** or **die Wortfolge**) is very similar—on the surface. However, whereas English sentences can sometimes be thrown together, German sentences have a specific word order and rules governing which words go where.

Die Wortfolge in Aussagesätzen (*Word order in statements*)

Regular sentence structure is subject—verb—the rest.

> Ich habe eine Katze.

Adding more elements complicates the mix: subject—verb—indirect object—adverb (time, manner, place)—direct object—infinitive verb—(separable prefix).

> Ich schenke meiner Mutter morgen vor der Schule zu Hause einen Blumenstrauß.

Usually though, in order to bring spice into a German sentence, something other than the subject will be in the first position, therefore allowing the speaker to emphasize another element in the sentence. The major rule to live by is that the majority of the time, the conjugated verb will be in the second position.

ÜBUNG
42·1

Satzbau. *Build correct regular sentences (subject first) using the cues provided.*

1. mein Vater / einen Rasenmäher / kauft / morgen

_____

2. die Blumen / unsere Mutter / gießt / am Nachmittag

_____

3. nach der Schule / wir / in ein Café / gehen

_____

4. ins Kino gehen / meine Freunde / wollen / und / heute Abend / einen Film schauen

_____

5. wir / am Wochenende / basteln / ein Modellauto

_____

6. vor dem Training / ich / nichts / essen / soll

_____

7. uns / Sie / sehen / bis nächste Woche / nicht

_____

ÜBUNG
42·2

Satzbau. *Build correct sentences that answer the question and that emphasize the boldfaced cue provided.*

1. Wann gehen wir ins Kino? **um 19 Uhr**

_____

2. Wo essen wir ein Eis? **im Café**

_____

3. Wie fahren wir nach Hause? **mit dem Rad**

_____

4. Was schenken wir Oma zum Geburtstag? **einen Blumenstrauß**

_____

5. Wem geben wir das Geschenk? **unseren Eltern**

_____

6. Wen sehen wir nach der Schule? **meinen Freund Axel**

_____

7. Wann kannst du am Wochenende mit mir Tennis spielen? **am Sonntag**

_____

8. Wohin fährt die Familie Schmitt in den Ferien? **nach Griechenland**

_____

ÜBUNG
42·3

Adverbien. *Put an X in the right category for each adverb: time (**T**), manner (**M**), or place (**P**).*

	T	M	P
1. heute	_____	_____	_____
2. nach Hause	_____	_____	_____
3. mit dem Zug	_____	_____	_____
4. nach der Schule	_____	_____	_____
5. um acht Uhr	_____	_____	_____
6. schnell	_____	_____	_____
7. am Abend	_____	_____	_____
8. nach Florida	_____	_____	_____
9. später	_____	_____	_____
10. zu Hause	_____	_____	_____

Die Wortfolge in Fragen (Word order in questions)

There are two types of questions—questions asking for information, and those asking for a yes or no answer.

Wann gehst du in die Schule?   *When are you going to school?*
Gehst du in die Schule?   *Are you going to school?*

Questions that ask for simple yes or no answers look just like a statement, except that the subject and verb are reversed. The verb comes first, and the subject goes in the second position. Questions that ask for information follow this word order: Question word—verb—subject—rest of question.

ÜBUNG
42·4

Übersetzung. *Translate the following questions.*

1. Do you (sing., informal) play tennis?

_____

2. Does she eat meat?

_____

3. Is he doing his homework?

_____

4. Is that a mouse?

_____

5. Are we going to school?

_____

6. Do they ski?

_____

7. Are we cooking tonight?

_____

ÜBUNG
42·5

Übersetzung. *Translate the following questions.*

1. When are we going downtown?

_____

2. Who did not do the homework?

_____

3. Where is the concert?

_____

4. Why can't we stay home?

_____

5. To whom are you (sing., informal) sending that letter?

_____

6. When does English class start?

_____

7. How often do you (sing., informal) feed the cat?

_____

8. Who is calling us this late?

_____

9. Where do you (sing.,informal) work?

_____

10. What do you (sing.,informal) want to do tonight?

_____

Word order— coordinating conjunctions

·43·

Koordinierende Konjunktionen (Coordinating conjunctions)

Coordinating conjunctions bring two independent sentences together to make one big complicated sentence. Because these two sentences are independent sentences that could also stand on their own, there is no change in the word order. The verb in the clause with the coordinating conjunction will remain in the second position.

Ich lese Bücher. Ich schaue Filme. Ich lese Bücher, und ich schaue Filme.

I read books. I watch movies. I read books, and I watch movies.

WORTSCHATZ

Koordinierende Konjunktionen (Coordinating conjunctions)

aber	but/however
denn	because
oder	or
sondern	rather
und	and

ÜBUNG
43·1

Combine the following sentences using the conjunctions provided.

1. (aber) Ich möchte schwimmen gehen. Es ist kalt.

   _____

2. (und) Meine Freunde sind nett. Sie sind auch schön.

   _____

3. (sondern) Er möchte nicht ins Kino gehen. Er will zu Hause bleiben.

   _____

4. (oder) Meine Familie isst zu Weihnachten Gans. Wir essen Ente.

_____

5. (aber) Wir spielen Golf. Ihr spielt Tennis.

_____

6. (sondern) Er trinkt keine Milch. Er trinkt lieber Cola.

_____

7. (denn) Wir lernen heute Abend. Wir haben morgen einen Test.

_____

8. (denn) Du kommst nicht mit. Du bist krank.

_____

9. (oder) Die Mädchen singen. Sie spielen Gitarre.

_____

10. (und) Meine Mutter arbeitet. Mein Vater bleibt zu Hause.

_____

Word order— subordinate clauses

A subordinate clause is one that cannot stand alone and is dependent on the main (or independent) clause. There are two main types of subordinate clauses—those that are introduced by a subordinating conjunction and relative clauses. For either kind of clause it is important to remember that the conjugated verb in the subordinate clause goes to the very end of the phrase in which it is found.

WORTSCHATZ

Subordinierende Konjunktionen (*Subordinating conjunctions*)

als	when (past)	**obwohl**	although
bevor	before	**seit(dem)**	since
bis	until	**sobald**	as soon as
da	since/because	**so dass**	so that
damit	so that	**solang(e)**	as long as
dass	that	**trotzdem**	despite
falls	in case	**während**	while
nachdem	after	**wann**	when (specific time)
ob	whether/if	**weil**	because
obgleich/obschon	although (uncommon)	**wenn**	if (conditional)

Die Wortfolge in Nebensätzen (*Word order in subordinate clauses*)

Subordinate clause in first position: Wann wir ins Kino gehen, weiß ich nicht.
Subordinate clause in final position: Ich weiß nicht, wann wir ins Kino gehen.

Sätze schreiben (*Write sentences*).

1. (weil) Magda kann nicht ins Kino gehen. Sie muss zu Hause helfen.

   _____

2. (als) Ich war nur vier Jahre alt. Ich konnte schon Fahrrad fahren.

   _____

3. (bis) Wir können nicht essen. Das Essen ist fertig.

   _____

4. (wenn) Ich hätte eine Million Dollar. Ich würde ein großes Haus kaufen.

   _____

5. (während) Meine Eltern sind weg. Ich bin alleine zu Hause.

   _____

6. (damit) Mein Cousin macht einen Kurs. Er kann Elektriker werden.

   _____

7. (nachdem) Sie gehen ein Eis essen. Sie haben den Film gesehen.

   _____

8. (bevor) Wir bringen die Gartenmöbel herein. Es wird dunkel.

   _____

9. (da) Sofia kauft den Mantel nicht. Sie hat nicht genug Geld.

   _____

10. (dass) Weißt du? Die Post ist um die Ecke.

    _____

Relativsätze (*Relative clauses*)

Relative clauses relate back to a noun in the main clause.

> *I know the man who stole the purse.*

Here the *who* refers back to the man who stole the purse.

> Ich kenne den Mann, der die Handtasche gestohlen hat.

die Relativpronomen (*Relative pronouns*)

	MASCULINE	FEMININE	NEUTER	PLURAL
Nominative	der	die	das	die
Accusative	den	die	das	die
Dative	dem	der	dem	denen
Genitive	dessen	deren	dessen	deren

ÜBUNG

44·2

Lücken ausfüllen. (*Fill in the blanks.*) *Fill in the blank with the correct relative pronoun.*

1. Wo ist der Mann, _____ Vegetarier ist?

2. Siehst du die Frau, _____ zu schnell fährt?

3. Hier ist ein Mädchen, _____ ich seit fünf Jahren kenne.

4. Später lernst du meine Großeltern kennen, _____ schon über 50 Jahren verheiratet sind.

5. Das ist der Junge, _____ ich auf dem Ball angesprochen habe.

6. Findest du den Ball, _____ ich beim Baseballspiel gefangen habe?

7. Wo ist das Kind, _____ wir gestern ein großes Geschenk gaben?

8. Wo sind die Eltern, _____ Kind hier alleine herumläuft?

9. Mein Freund mag Häuser nicht, in _____ man nicht aufrecht stehen kann.

10. Hast du ein Stück Papier, _____ ich haben könnte?

ÜBUNG

44·3

Sätze schreiben. (*Write sentences.*) *Use relative pronouns to connect the sentences.*

1. Wo ist die Tasche? Ich habe sie gestern gekauft.

_____

2. Meine Eltern kennen einen Mann. Er ist Weltmeister in Fußball.

_____

3. Siehst du die Frau? Ihre Mutter ist gestorben.

_____

4. Hier ist ein Kuli. Du kannst ihn borgen.

_____

5. Wir haben einen Film gesehen. Er war stinklangweilig.

_____

6. Hier ist ein Mädchen. Ich helfe ihm.

_____

7. Kennst du die Frau? Ihr Freund hat ihr einen Blumenstrauß gegeben.

_____

8. Mein Bruder ist ein Mensch. Man kann mit ihm gut Schach spielen.

_____

9. Der Fluß heißt die Oder. Er fließt durch Frankfurt.

_____

10. Deutsch ist ein Fach. Das Fach macht Spaß.

_____

Infinitive phrases—zu  **·45·**

Das Infinitiv (*The Infinitive*)

When a sentence has more than one verb in it, only one of them will be conjugated and the other verbs are placed at the end of the sentence, in their infinitive form. **Hinweis** (*Note*): If the English sentence includes the preposition *to* before the infinitive, the equivalent German sentence will include the preposition **zu** before the equivalent German infinitive. Also, if an infinitive verb contains a separable prefix, the **zu** must be inserted between the prefix and the main verb: **mitzunehmen**.

I plan to go to college.   Ich habe vor, auf die Uni zu gehen.

ÜBUNG
45·1

Unsere Pläne (*Our plans*). *Complete the following sentences.*

1. Thomas möchte nach Frankreich fahren.

   Thomas plant _____

2. Wir wollen einen schönen Urlaub machen.

   Wir haben vor _____

3. Meine Eltern möchten ein Haus kaufen.

   Meine Eltern planen _____

4. Stefanie möchte viel Geld verdienen.

   Stefanie hat vor _____

5. Alles ist in Ordnung.

   Alles scheint _____

6. Emma will die Hausaufgaben machen.

   Emma schlägt vor _____

7. Wir nehmen einen Regenschirm mit.

   Wir planen _____

8. Hans möchte die See sehen.

   Hans hat vor _____

9. Wir wollen Spaß haben.

   Wir haben vor _____

10. Mein Vater will nicht, dass ich abends spät nach Hause komme.

    Papa verbietet mir _____

Sometimes the infinitive construction is used when two separate activities take place (or don't take place) simultaneously. **Zu** can be used following prepositions such as **(an)statt, außer, ohne**, and **um**.

ÜBUNG

45·2

Immer das Gegenteil (*Always the opposite*). *Write sentences with the given cues by starting the sentences with* **statt**.

1. zuhören—sie macht was sie will

   _____

2. langsamer fahren—sie rast auf der Autobahn

   _____

3. genug Geld mitnehmen—sie kann nichts kaufen

   _____

4. mit den Eltern in Urlaub fahren—sie bleibt in den Ferien zu Hause

   _____

5. schauen—sie fährt einfach los

   _____

Cardinal and ordinal numbers
The calendar: months, seasons, days of the week

·46·

WORTSCHATZ

Die Grundzahlen (*Cardinal numbers*)

0	null	21	einundzwanzig
1	eins	22	zweiundzwanzig
2	zwei	23	dreiundzwanzig
3	drei	24	vierundzwanzig
4	vier	25	fünfundzwanzig
5	fünf	26	sechsundzwanzig
6	sechs	27	siebenundzwanzig
7	sieben	28	achtundzwanzig
8	acht	29	neunundzwanzig
9	neun	30	dreißig
10	zehn	40	vierzig
11	elf	50	fünfzig
12	zwölf	60	sechzig
13	dreizehn	70	siebzig
14	vierzehn	80	achtzig
15	fünfzehn	90	neunzig
16	sechzehn	100	(ein)hundert
17	siebzehn	101	hunderteins
18	achtzehn	120	hundertzwanzig
19	neunzehn	200	zweihundert
20	zwanzig	999	neunhundertneunundneunzig

1.000	tausend
1.001	tausendeins
10.000	zehntausend
100.000	hunderttausend
1.000.000	eine Million
1.000.000.000	eine Milliarde
1.000.000.000.000	eine Billion

In German, there is either a space or a period in the position where a comma would normally be in English. Numbers are feminine.

Welche Zahl ist das? *For each number, write out the word.*

1. die 5 _____

2. die 3 _____

3. die 10 _____

4. die 100 _____

5. die 56 _____

6. die 65 _____

7. die 90 _____

8. die 33 _____

9. die 52 _____

10. die 87 _____

11. die 1.000.000 _____

12. die 1.999 _____

Wie viel Uhr ist es? (*What time is it?*) *Label each time by writing out the words.*

1. 15.00 _____

2. 8.05 _____

3. 20.55 _____

4. 2.22 _____

5. 10.17 _____

6. 1.48 _____

7. 21.09 _____

8. 9.21 _____

9. 5.02 _____

10. 6.35 _____

Die Ordnungszahlen (*Ordinal numbers*)

To create an ordinal number, take the cardinal number and add **-te** (for the numbers 1 through 19) or **-ste** (for the numbers 20 and up) to the ending. Some numbers will drop a few letters (**sieben—siebte**), or the word will completely change (**eins—erste**). The ending is an adjective ending and must be adapted to both the noun it modifies and the case of the noun. To shorten the written form of the numbers, simply use the numeral with a period after it.

Hinweis (*Note*): Notice that the date is written day/month/year.

Heute ist der 4. Mai. | *Today is May 4th.*

| WORTSCHATZ |

Die Ordnungszahlen (*Ordinal numbers*)

1. der erste		21. der einundzwanzigste	
2. der zweite		22. der zweiundzwanzigste	
3. der dritte		23. der dreiundzwanzigste	
4. der vierte		24. der vierundzwanzigste	
5. der fünfte		25. der fünfundzwanzigste	
6. der sechste		26. der sechsundzwanzigste	
7. der siebte		27. der siebenundzwanzigste	
8. der achte		28. der achtundzwanzigste	
9. der neunte		29. der neunundzwanzigste	
10. der zehnte		30. der dreißigste	
11. der elfte		40. der vierzigste	
12. der zwölfte		50. der fünfzigste	
13. der dreizehnte		60. der sechzigste	
14. der vierzehnte		70. der siebzigste	
15. der fünfzehnte		80. der achtzigste	
16. der sechzehnte		90. der neunzigste	
17. der siebzehnte		100. der hundertste	
18. der achtzehnte			
19. der neunzehnte			
20. der zwanzigste			

| WORTSCHATZ |

Der Kalender

Die Monate (Maskulin)

Januar	January	**Juli**	July
Februar	February	**August**	August
März	March	**September**	September
April	April	**Oktober**	October
Mai	May	**November**	November
Juni	June	**Dezember**	December

Die Jahreszeiten (Maskulin)

Frühling (das Frühjahr, im Frühling)	spring	**Sommer (im Sommer)**	summer
Herbst (im Herbst)	autumn	**Winter (im Winter)**	winter

Die Tage der Woche (Maskulin)

Montag	Monday
Dienstag	Tuesday
Mittwoch	Wednesday
Donnerstag	Thursday
Freitag	Friday
Samstag	Saturday
Sonnabend	(Saturday: eastern and northern Germany)
Sonntag	Sunday

Hinweis (*Note*): When saying that something happens on a particular day, write **am** before the name of the day (**am Samstag**).

ÜBUNG
46·3

An welchem Wochentag macht man das? (*What day of the week do you do that on?*) *Write the day (or days) of the week when the following events usually occur.*

1. Ich lerne nicht, denn ich habe keine Schule. _____ und _____

2. das Meisterschaftsspiel im amerikanischen Profifootball _____

3. der Beginn der Arbeitswoche _____

4. wann Christen in die Kirche gehen _____

5. der erste Tag vom Wochenende _____

6. der zweite Tag nach Sonntag _____

ÜBUNG
46·4

Wann feiert man das? (*What date is each holiday celebrated on?*) *(Hint: don't forget that dates are written in the order day/month in German.)*

1. Weihnachten (*Christmas*)? Das ist _____.

2. Tag der deutschen Einheit (3.10.)? Das ist _____.

3. der Unabhängigkeitstag in den USA (4.7.)? Das ist _____.

4. Halloween? Das ist _____.

5. Heilige Drei Könige (6.1.)? Das ist _____.

6. Nikolaus (6.12.)? Das ist _____.

7. Allerheiligen (1.11.)? Das ist _____.

8. Neujahr (1.1.)? Das ist _____.

9. Valentinstag? Das ist _____.

10. der erste Herbsttag? Das ist _____.

In welchem Monat ist das? (*What month is that in?*)

1. In welchem Monat ist Boxing Day in Kanada? _____

2. Wann ist die Schule normalerweise zu Ende? _____

3. Wann feiert man Weihnachten? _____

4. Wann beginnt Chanukka? _____

5. Wann feiert man Valentinstag? _____

6. Wann beginnt normalerweise das Schuljahr? _____

   oder _____

7. Wann ist es in Griechenland sehr heiß? _____

   und _____

8. Wann ist es in Wisconsin sehr kalt? _____ und

   _____

9. Wann ist es in der nördlichen Erdhälfte (*Northern Hemisphere*)

   Frühling? _____, _____,

   _____, und _____

10. Wann ist Muttertag? _____

Spaßfakten (*Fun facts*)

Die Originalordnungszahl (*The original ordinal number*)

Georg Cantor erfand 1897 die Ordnungszahl. Cantor war deutscher Mathemathiker. Er wurde in Russland geboren. Ordunungszahlen definieren die Beziehung (*relationship*) zwischen den Grundzahlen. Sie können nicht im Negativen auftreten.

Answer key

1·1   1. post 2. ball 3. run 4. watch 5. quiet

2·1   1. läuft 2. Maus 3. Bein 4. Euro

2·2   1. Stur 2. Rock 3. Quelle

3·1   1. der Frau 2. des Mannes 3. das Haus 4. dem Mann 5. der Frau

3·2   1. einer Frau 2. eines Mannes 3. ein Haus 4. einem Mann 5. einer Frau

4·1   1. die 2. der 3. das 4. das 5. die 6. die 7. das 8. die 9. die 10. der

4·2   1. der 2. die 3. Die 4. Das 5. Die 6. Der 7. die 8. Das

4·3   1. den Baum 2. das Feld 3. den Schnee 4. die Wolke 5. die Blumen

4·4   1. diesen 2. dieses 3. dieses 4. diese 5. dieses 6. diesen

4·5   1. Ich möchte jenes (dieses) Auto.   2. Welchem Mädchen kauft er die Blumen?
        3. Solche Häuser sind teuer.   4. Jedes Buch ist gut.   5. Alle Blumen sind schön.
        6. Manche Wolken sind nicht weiß.

5·1   1. ein 2. eine 3. eine 4. Ein 5. Ein

5·2   1. einen Kuli 2. einen Computer 3. eine CD 4. einen Radiergummi 5. eine
        Schere 6. einen Bleistift 7. einen Buntstift 8. eine Heftmaschine

6·1   1. Der Autobus 2. Das Lieblingsbuch 3. Das Hochhaus 4. Das Schlafzimmer
        5. Die Straßenlampe

7·1   1. die Garagen 2. die Keller 3. die Türen 4. die Gärten 5. die Gänge

7·2   1. Zimmer 2. Fenster 3. Lampen 4. Stühle 5. Bäume 6. Blumen
        7. Autos 8. Haustiere

8·1

1. spiele	spielst	spielt	spielen	spielt	spielen
2. sage	sagst	sagt	sagen	sagt	sagen
3. mache	machst	macht	machen	macht	machen
4. gehe	gehst	geht	gehen	geht	gehen
5. schaue	schaust	schaut	schauen	schaut	schauen
6. höre	hörst	hört	hören	hört	hören
7. koche	kochst	kocht	kochen	kocht	kochen
8. springe	springst	springt	springen	springt	springen

9. lache	lachst	lacht	lachen	lacht	lachen
10. lerne	lernst	lernt	lernen	lernt	lernen

8·2 1. Ich springe. 2. Du sagst. 3. Sie sagt. 4. Sie lernen. 5. Ihr lernt. 6. Sie tanzen. 7. Wir tanzen. 8. Er kocht. 9. Wir kochen. 10. Es tanzt. 11. Er hört. 12. Du hörst. 13. Sie schauen. 14. Ich spiele. 15. Es spielt. 16. Wir gehen.

8·3 1. SN (Ich lerne Deutsch.) 2. SN (Wir tanzen in der Disko.) 3. SN (Eis kann man nicht kochen.) 4. S

9·1 1. Ich kaufe das Buch. Ich kaufe es. 2. Er hat einen Stuhl. Er hat ihn. 3. Sie kauft den Mantel. Sie kauft ihn. 4. Wir sehen die Katze. Wir sehen sie. 5. Sie hören die Mädchen. Sie hören sie. 6. Wir sehen euch. 7. Der Junge mag dich.

9·2 1. Ich habe die Bücher. Ich habe sie. 2. Wir haben die Autos. Wir haben sie. 3. Sie sehen die Blumen. Sie sehen sie.

9·3 1. toy, him 2. pen, student 3. letter, you 4. story, us 5. card, me 6. lie, girl 7. book, child 8. present, me

9·4 1. Wir schenken ihm ein Buch. 2. Sie schenkt mir ein Geschenk. 3. Du schenkst uns die Mäntel. 4. Sie schenken dir die Blumen. 5. Ich schenke ihr die Katze. 6. Wir schenken ihnen den Taschenrechner. 7. Er schenkt euch das Papier. 8. Ich schenke Ihnen das Haus.

10·1 1. Das ist mein Vater. Das ist meine Mutter. Das sind meine Eltern. 2. Das ist ihre Schwester. Das ist ihr Bruder. Das sind ihre Geschwister. 3. Das ist dein Haustier. Das ist deine Katze. 4. Das sind unsere Großeltern. Das ist unsere Großmutter. Das ist unser Großvater.

10·2 1. unser Vater 2. ihre Großmutter 3. deine Geschwister 4. meine Halbschwester 5. seine Mutter 6. Ihr Großvater 7. euer Stiefbruder 8. ihr Cousin

10·3 1. meinen Vater 2. seine Schwester 3. unseren Großvater 4. ihre Eltern 5. ihren Onkel

10·4 1. ihrs 2. deiner 3. meiner 4. seine 5. ihrs 6. euers

10·5 1. unseren 2. meiner 3. ihrem 4. eurem 5. seiner

10·6 1. ihrer 2. meiner 3. eurer 4. ihres 5. seines

11·1 1. Ich beeile mich. 2. Wir freuen uns. 3. Sie erholen sich. 4. Du erkältest dich. 5. Er gewöhnt sich an die Schule. 6. Sie freut sich auf die Party. 7. Ich erinnere mich an das Haus.

11·2 1. sich 2. sich 3. uns 4. mir 5. sich 6. dir 7. euch 8. mir

11·3 1. Max erholt sich jedes Wochenende. 2. Jana interessiert sich für Eishockey. 3. Wir rasieren uns jeden Morgen. 4. Ihr freut euch auf die Party 5. Ich putze mir die Zähne.

12·1 1. Das da. 2. Die da. 3. Der da. 4. Das da. 5. Den da. 6. Das da. 7. Denen da.

12·2 1. diesen 2. dieses 3. dieses 4. diese 5. diese

13·1 1. Jeder 2. jedem 3. jeden 4. niemand(en) 5. Niemand 6. niemand(em) 7. Man 8. einen 9. einem

13·2 1. nichts 2. Jemand 3. Alle 4. einige 5. Mehrere 6. manchen 7. etwas

14·1 1. Wen 2. wen 3. wem 4. Wer 5. Wer 6. Wessen 7. wen 8. Wessen

14·2 1. Was 2. Wer 3. Wer 4. Was 5. Wer 6. Was

14·3 1. Welches Haus ist das? 2. Welcher Schüler ist das? 3. Welchen Lehrer haben wir? (Welchen Lehrer habt ihr?) 4. Welche Musik gefällt dir? 5. An welche Universität gehst du?

14·4 1. Wie viel 2. Wie viele 3. wie vielen 4. Wie viel 5. wie vielen 6. Wie viele 7. Wie viele 8. Wie viele

15·1   1. Ich bin groß.   2. Er ist dünn.   3. Wir sind reich.   4. Sie sind nett.   5. Seid ihr glücklich?   6. Sie sind hübsch.   7. Das Auto ist schnell.   8. Der Tisch ist häßlich.   9. Mein Onkel ist dick.   10. Superman ist nicht böse.

15·2   1. gute Freunde haben   2. sichere Einkunft haben   3. in schönen Urlaub fahren   4. mit eigenen Kindern spielen   5. tolle Speisen essen   6. gutes Geld verdienen   7. trotz kleiner Probleme glücklich sein

15·3   1. guter   2. amerikanisches   3. schlechtem   4. große   5. guter   6. schwerem   7. schlechtes

16·1   1. Dieses Auto ist schneller.   2. Ihre Haare sind lockiger.   3. Dieses Haus ist kleiner.   4. Diese Heftmaschine ist älter.   5. Dieser Bleistift ist länger.

16·2   1. Der Berg ist höher.   2. Das Essen ist hier besser.   3. Ich trinke jetzt mehr Wasser.

16·3   1. schneller   2. größer   3. dunkel   4. mehr   5. teurer   6. hoch   7. langweilig   8. alt

16·4   1. Dieses Auto ist am schnellsten.   2. Ihre Haare sind am lockigsten.   3. Dieses Haus ist am kleinsten.   4. Diese Heftmaschine ist am ältesten.   5. Dieser Bleistift ist am längsten.

16·5   1. Ich bin groß. Meine Schwester ist größer. Meine Mutter ist am größten.   2. Der VW ist teuer. Der BMW ist teurer. Der Audi ist am teuersten.   3. Das Fahrrad ist schnell. Das Auto ist schneller. Der Zug ist am schnellsten.   4. Sein Vater ist alt. Sein Onkel ist älter. Sein Großvater ist am ältesten.

17·1   1. das große Haus   2. das warme Essen   3. der kleine Garten   4. der grüne Kopfsalat   5. das kalte Wasser   6. der schwarze Kaffee   7. die grüne Banane   8. die saftigen Erdbeeren   9. das gebackene Fleisch   10. der alte Apfel

17·2   1. Ich esse gern grüne Trauben.   2. Ich trinke kaltes Wasser nach dem Sport.   3. Ich trinke keinen Kaffee.   4. Meine Mutter trinkt gern heißen Tee mit Milch.   5. Die Jungen essen nicht gern Meeresfrüchte.   6. Meine Schwester isst nicht gern grüne Trauben.   7. Isst du jeden Tag einen roten Apfel?   8. Gute Kinder trinken viel Wasser.   9. Sie essen nicht gern grüne Eier und kalten Schinken.   10. Ich trinke am Morgen ein großes Glas Milch.

17·3   1. meiner jungen Kusine/meinem jungen Cousin   2. eine neue Uhr   3. unserer alten Mathelehrerin/unseres alten Mathelehrers   4. Die deutsche Kanzlerin/Der deutsche Kanzler   5. fünf Bücher und einen häßlichen Pullover   6. dem großen Supermarkt   7. neben dem kleinen Park vor dem schöen Schloss

18·1   1. Wir bauen ein Haus.   2. Das Mädchen studiert Deutsch.   3. Sie zahlen.   4. Ihr wechselt euer Geld.   5. Er lebt (wohnt) in Deutschland.   6. Wir tanzen Walzer.   7. Das Essen schmeckt gut.   8. Meine Kinder üben ihre Musik.   9. Meine Mutter wandert.   10. Ich koche und reise.

18·2   1. Ich koche.   2. Ich lache.   3. Ich huste.   4. Ich besuche.   5. Ich packe.   6. Ich fliege.   7. Ich heirate. / Wir heiraten.   8. Ich putze.   9. Ich verdiene.   10. Ich wechsele mein Geld.

19·1   1. du fängst, er/sie/es fängt   2. du brichst, er/sie/es bricht   3. du empfiehlst, er/sie/es empfiehlt   4. du isst, er/sie/es isst   5. du gibst, er/sie/es gibt   6. du lässt, er/sie/es lässt   7. du liest, er/sie/es liest   8. du nimmst, er/sie/es nimmt   9. du schläfst, er/sie/es schläft   10. du siehst, er/sie/es sieht

19·2   1. Ich heiße Svenja.   2. Sie trinken Milch.   3. Wir bleiben hier.   4. Der Vogel fliegt.   5. Du kommst aus Florida.   6. Er fängt den Ball.   7. Meine Mutter schreibt einen Brief.

20·1   1. fliegst, ab   2. trinken, aus   3. isst, auf   4. nehmen, mit   5. lebe, ein   6. probiert, an   7. Kommt, mit

20·2   1. Die Schule fängt um acht Uhr an.   2. Die Schuhe sehen gut aus.   3. Der Zug kommt nicht pünktlich an.   4. Mir fällt nichts ein.   5. Meine Eltern fahren im Auto mit.   6. Die Schüler fahren als Klasse in die Schweiz weg.   7. Der Vater deckt das schlafende Kind zu.

20·3   1. Die Schüler beantworten die Frage.   2. Wir verstehen die Anleitung nicht.   3. Das Auto versagt in der Wüste.   4. Der Lehrer vergisst die Aufgaben zu Hause.   5. Die Eltern versprechen nichts.

V

21·1   1. habe   2. Haben   3. haben   4. hat   5. Habt   6. haben   7. hast

21·2   1. Ich habe ein Pferd.   2. Ich habe keinen Wolf.   3. Wir haben zwei Katzen.   4. Meine Schwester hat kein Huhn.   5. Sie haben einige (ein paar) Hunde.   6. Ihr habt Enten.   7. Er hat keine Mäuse.   8. Frau Thomas, Sie haben einen Fisch.

21·3   1. Z   2. Z   3. H   4. B   5. Z   6. H   7. B   8. H   9. B   10. B   11. H   12. B   13. B

Germany and animals

There are almost 700 zoological gardens, wildlife preserves, aquariums, bird parks, and animal reservations in Germany.

There are 414 zoos.

Berlin's "Zoologischer Garten" (zoological garden) is the largest in the world and contains 1,500 different species and 14,000 animals.

German shepherds have the best noses in the dog world, which is why they are trained as police dogs. Why the good nose? They have 225 million cell receptors in their noses.

German shepherds originally herded groups of animals.

The first man who bred a German shepherd was Max von Stephanitz. The first puppy in the second generation was Beowulf, who became the ancestor of all German shepherds. The German shepherd was first bred in 1899.

For a short time, German shepherds were called Alsatians *in English because the name "German" shepherd was problematic after the Second World War.*

22·1   1. sind   2. ist   3. ist   4. sind   5. ist   6. sind   7. seid

22·2   1. SN   2. S.   3. SN   4. S   5. S   6. SN   7. S   8. S

22·3   1. Ich bin Elektriker/in.   2. Sie ist Polizistin.   3. Er ist Hausmann.   4. Wir sind Lehrer.   5. Ihr seid Ärzte.   6. Sie sind Klempner.

23·1   1. werden   2. werden   3. werde   4. wird   5. Werdet   6. werden   7. Wirst

23·2   1. ein Tierarzt   2. eine Apothekerin   3. ein Spion   4. eine Köchin   5. ein Gärtner   6. einen Schaupieler

23·3   1. S   2. SN   3. S   4. S   5. SN   6. SN   7. SN   8. S

23·4   1. Ihr werdet Feuerwehrmänner/Feuerwehrfrauen/Feuerwehrleute.   2. Sie werden Gärtner/Gärtnerinnen.   3. Sie wird Metzgerin.   4. Er wird Journalist.   5. Ich werde Spion/Spionin.   6. Du wirst Tierarzt/Tierärztin.   7. Wir werden Mechaniker/Mechanikerinnen.   8. Ich werde Koch/Köchin.

24·1   1. Meine Familie will ein Haus bauen.   2. Ihre Schwester darf nicht Auto fahren.   3. Der Mann kann nicht hören.   4. Wir sollen Abendessen kochen.   5. Du musst deine Hausaufgaben machen.   6. Es möchte etwas fressen.   7. Dürft ihr ins Kino gehen?

25·1   1. Weißt   2. Wisst   3. Wissen   4. Weiß   5. Wissen   6. Weiß

25·2   1. S   2. S   3. SN   4. S   5. SN   6. S

25·3   1. E   2. C   3. D   4. F   5. A   6. B

25·4   1. S   2. S   3. S   4. SN   5. SN   6. S   7. SN

25·5   1. Ich kenne einige Leute.   2. Mein Elektriker kennt meinen Mann.   3. Unser Tierarzt kennt viele Familien.   4. Wir kennen Seattle sehr gut.   5. Er kennt die Schüler/Studenten.

VI

26·1   1. erhole mich, erholst dich, erholt sich, erholen uns, erholt euch, erholen sich

2. wasche mich/mir, wäscht dich/dir, wäscht sich, waschen uns, wascht euch, waschen sich

3. stelle mir vor, stellst dir vor, stellt sich vor, stellen uns vor, stellt euch vor, stellen sich vor

4. rasiere mich/mir, rasierst dich/dir, rasiert sich, rasieren uns, rasiert euch, rasieren sich

5. verspäte mich, verspätest dich, verspätet sich, verspäten uns, verspätet euch, verspäten sich

6. erkälte mich, erkältest dich, erkältet sich, erkälten uns, erkältet euch, erkälten sich

7. beeile mich, beeilst dich, beeilt sich, beeilen uns, beeilt euch, beeilen sich

8. setze mich, setzt dich, setzt sich, setzen uns, setzt euch, setzen sich

9. entscheide mich, entscheidest dich, entscheidet sich, entsheiden uns, entscheidet euch, entscheiden sich

10. tue mir weh, tust dir weh, tut sich weh, tun uns weh, tut euch weh, tun sich weh

26·2 1. Wir amüsieren uns jedes Wochenende. 2. Sie setzen sich. 3. Er rasiert sich jeden Morgen. 4. Ihr werdet euch erkälten! 5. Herr Sturm, Sie sollen sich erholen. 6. Sie muss sich jetzt entscheiden. 7. Du tust dir das Bein weh. 8. Ich kann mich nicht beeilen. 9. Sie müssen sich anziehen.

26·3 1. Sam beeilt sich jeden Morgen. 2. Wir interessieren uns für Sport. 3. Er entschuldigt sich bei mir. 4. Das Kind fürchtet sich vor dem Sturm. 5. Die Kinder waschen sich. 6. Ihr wascht euch die Gesichter. 7. Ich rege mich über meine schlechte Note auf.

Personal hygiene
- *Germans do not always shower every day.*
- *Body scent is something natural, not something bad.*
- *Some older women do not shave either their legs or their underarms.*
- *People often go naked into German saunas.*
- *During a visit to the doctor's office, you undress completely, but the doctor stays in the room the entire time!*

27·1 1. Mach die Hausaufgabe! 2. Schenken wir ihr einen Blumenstrauß! 3. Holt ein Buch aus der Bibliothek! 4. Fahren wir in die Stadt! 5. Kaufen Sie einen neuen Wagen! 6. Geh in die Schule! 7. Sehen wir einen Film! 8. Nehmen Sie die Klasse mit! 9. Geht ins Kino! 10. Schlaf ein!

27·2 1. Kauf das Brot beim Bäcker! 2. Holt das Fleisch beim Metzger! 3. Fragen Sie den Mann! 4. Geben Sie mir den Kuli! 5. Kaufen wir die Milch im Supermarkt! 6. Fangen wir an! 7. Trink ein bisschen Wasser! 8. Trinkt keinen Kaffee!

27·3 1. F/A 2. M 3. M 4. F/A 5. F 6. F 7. F

27·4 1. Seien 2. Sei 3. Seien 4. Seid 5. Sei 6. Seien

28·1 1. W 2. K 3. K 4. B 5. K/B 6. W 7. W

28·2 1. S 2. H 3. S 4. H 5. S 6. S 7. H 8. H 9. S 10. H 11. S 12. H 13. H

28·3 1. Ilse hat den ersten Preis bekommen. 2. Meine Eltern sind am Wochenende gekommen. 3. Wir haben keine Hausaufgaben gehabt. 4. Boris Becker hat Tennis gespielt. 5. Ihr habt am Sonntag lange geschlafen. 6. Frau Hennes, Sie haben viel über Chemie gewusst. 7. Ich habe meine Freundin angerufen. 8. Wir sind in die Berge gefahren. 9. Der Hans hat eine Geschichte erzählt. 10. Mein Lehrer ist nach Ägypten geflogen.

29·1 1. Ich lernte viel. 2. Frau Müller rauchte. 3. Das Kind weinte. 4. Atmetest du? 5. Wir öffneten die Tür. 6. Die Jungen wohnten hier. 7. Arbeitetet ihr? 8. Das Mädchen lächelte. 9. Ich wohnte in Frankfurt. 10. Was sagtest du?

29·2 1. Meine Eltern machten viel mit uns. 2. Wir reisten überall. 3. Ich machte selten mit meiner Familie Urlaub. 4. Meine Oma backte jeden Samstag Kuchen. 5. Mein Vater kochte einmal die Woche für uns. 6. Mein Bruder und ich schauten jeden Samstag Fernsehen. 7. Alle Kinder spielten ein Instrument. 8. Mähtet ihr auch einmal im Monat den Rasen? 9. Die Kusinen kauften immer CDs. 10. Ich putzte jedes Wochenende das Bad.

29·3 1. biss 2. aß 3. fand 4. gab 5. ging 6. gewann 7. hieß 8. half 9. kam 10. log 11. saß 12. sprach 13. tat

29·4 1. Oma brachte frische Petersilie aus ihrem Garten mit. 2. Er wusste, dass wir euch ein Päckchen sandten. 3. Wir benannten das Baby. 4. Kanntest du die Familie? 5. Brachten wir etwas mit zur Fete? 6. Ich dachte nach. 7. Die Kinder rannten aus dem Haus. 8. Sie wandte mir den Rücken.

29·5 1. Ich wollte das machen. 2. Du solltest zum Arzt gehen. 3. Wir konnten nicht Fahrrad fahren. 4. Sie wollte Eis. 5. Sie wollten ins Kino gehen. 6. Die Jungen durften nicht lange schlafen. 7. Maria konnte ein neues Kleid kaufen. 8. Konntest du ein bisschen Kuchen mitbringen?

30·1   1. waren   2. hatte   3. hatten   4. war   5. war   6. Hattet   7. hatten   8. hatte   9. war   10. hatten

30·2   1. hatte sie jeden Tag Fußball gespielt.   2. war sie im Schwimmbad geschwommen.   3. war sie in den Urlaub zum Bergsteigen geflogen.   4. hatte sie einen Marathon gelaufen.   5. hatte sie alles in den dritten Stockwerk getragen.   6. hatte sie mit Freunden einen Film im Kino gesehen.   7. war sie oft nach der Schule ins Kino gegangen.   8. hatte sie ihre Großeltern besucht.   9. hatte sie in der ganzen Wohnung Staub gesaugt.   10. hatte sie in der Disko getanzt.

31·1   1. Ich werde singen.   2. Wir werden essen.   3. Sie werden tanzen.   4. Sie wird die Antwort wissen.   5. Ihr werdet Basketball spielen.   6. Herr Schulz, werden Sie ins Kino gehen?   7. Was werden wir morgen machen?   8. Ich werde nichts machen.   9. Du wirst deine Hausaufgaben machen.   10. Sie werden in Deutschland wohnen.

31·2   1. Ich werde heute Abend um 22 Uhr ins Bett gehen.   2. Er wird sich morgen früh die Zähne putzen.   3. Wirst du später baden?   4. Nächste Woche werden wir heiraten.   5. Sie werden nächsten Monat ein Auto kaufen.   6. Ihr werdet übermorgen einen Test schreiben.   7. Ihr werdet heute Abend essen.

32·1   1. Bis neun Uhr werde ich drei Stunden lang Tennis gespielt haben.   2. Sie wird die ganze Nacht getanzt haben.   3. Sie werden zwei Stunden lang hier gesessen haben.   4. Wir werden bis nächstes Jahr das Haus gekauft haben.   5. Bevor er 21 wird wird er nach Europa gegangen sein.   6. Ihr werdet bis morgen die Hausaufgaben gemacht haben.   7. Sie werden bis Montag einkaufen gegangen sein.

33·1   1. werden, gemacht   2. wird, gefüttert   3. wird, sortiert   4. werden, gegossen   5. werden, gemacht   6. wird, gespült   7. wird, gemäht   8. wird, gedeckt   9. wird, abgeräumt   10. wird, aufgeräumt

33·2   1. Das Lied wurde gesungen.   2. Das Buch wird geschrieben.   3. Das Glas ist kaputt gemacht geworden.   4. Das Essen ist gegessen geworden.   5. Die Stühle wurden genommen.   6. Das Zimmer wird geputzt werden.   7. Die Zeitungen werden gelesen.   8. Die Kinder werden unterrichtet/gelehrt.   9. Deutsch wurde gelernt/studiert.   10. Die Spiele wurden gespielt.

34·1   1. Hätte   2. Wäre   3. Wäre   4. Hätten   5. Wäre   6. Hätte   7. Wäret

34·2   1. würde   2. würden   3. würden   4. würdet   5. würde   6. würden

34·3   1. Könnte   2. Dürfte   3. Spielte   4. Wollte   5. Hätte   6. Möchte   7. Wollte

"My hat"
My hat, it has three corners,
Three corners has my hat,
And had it not three corners,
then it would not be my hat.

35·1   1. Er sagt, er sage es nicht.   2. Sie sagt, sie habe es nicht.   3. Sie sagen, sie haben es nicht getan.   4. Sie sagt, sie sei nicht zu Hause.   5. Er sagt, er habe nichts gehört.   6. Sie sagen, sie wissen nicht, was passiert sei.   7. Sie sagt, das Land solle keinen Krieg führen.   8. Er sagt, der Autohersteller sei in diesem Fall schuldig.   9. Sie sagen, sie lebe schon seit 10 Jahren in der Stadt.   10. Sie sagen, der Schüler könne kein Türkisch sprechen.

36·1   1. Magic Johnson und Michael Jordan können gut Basketball spielen.   2. Maria Sharapova kann gut Tennis spielen.   3. Edgar Allan Poe kann gut schreiben.   4. Plácido Domingo kann gut singen.   5. Céline Dion kann gut singen.   6. Richard Petty kann gut fahren.   7. Ronaldo kann gut Fußball spielen.

36·2   1. b. oft   2. b. immer   3. c. drinnen   4. a. selten   5. a. immer   6. b. hinten   7. a. schnell

36·3   1. draußen   2. drinnen   3. oben   4. hier   5. hinten   6. überall   7. rechts

36·4   1. Warum warst du nicht auf der Party?   2. Was sieht sie?   3. Wohin gehen wir nach der Schule?   4. Wer soll die Frage beantworten?   5. Warum können wir nicht gehen?   6. Was macht er?   7. Wann können wir essen?   8. Wem schenkt/gibt er den Ring?   9. Wessen Schuhe sind das?   10. Wie viel kostet der Hund?

36·5   1. Was hat sie getragen?   2. Was hat er gegessen?   3. Wen haben wir/habt ihr gehört?   4. Wie viel hat das Auto gekostet?   5. Warum können wir/könnt ihr nicht gehen?   6. Wann gehen sie ins Kino?   7. Wer fährt nach Mexiko?   8. Wie läuft die Schildkröte?

37·1   1. um   2. für   3. bis   4. für   5. um   6. für   7. für   8. um

37·2   1. dich   2. wen   3. die Frau   4. ihn   5. das Haus   6. den Fluss   7. seinen Sohn   8. deinen   9. ihre Tante   10. den Saal

37·3   1. Die Party beginnt um acht Uhr.   2. Die Geschenke sind für dich.   3. Die Mädchen sind den Fluss entlang gelaufen.   4. Ich gehe ohne ein Buch nie aus dem Haus.   5. Unsere Schule spielt morgen gegen eine schlechte Mannschaft.   6. Wir müssen durch den Regen laufen.   7. Der Vogel ist gegen das Fenster geflogen.   8. Das Volk stimmt für den Präsidenten.   9. Sie mäht für ihre Eltern den Rasen.   10. Er arbeitet bis 17 Uhr.

38·1   1. bei   2. Mit   3. gegenüber   4. seit   5. zur   6. außer   7. aus   8. nach

38·2   1. dem Sofa   2. wem   3. mir   4. den Schülern   5. dem Haus   6. den Lehrern   7. dir   8. deinen   9. dem Abend   10. ihren Freunden

38·3   1. Ich gehe zur Universität.   2. Willst du mit mir einen Film sehen?   3. Seit gestern habe ich Kopfschmerzen.   4. Die Geschenke sind von uns.   5. Wir stehen ihm gegenüber.   6. Alle Kinder außer ihnen trinken Milch.   7. Die Jungen kommen aus der Schule.

39·1   1. außerhalb   2. jenseits   3. diesseits   4. oberhalb   5. innerhalb   6. trotz   7. wegen

39·2   1. des Mannes   2. der Stunde   3. des Mädchens   4. der Schule   5. der See   6. des Hauses   7. des Dorfes   8. des Saftes

40·1   1. K   2. S   3. S   4. K   5. S   6. K   7. K   8. K

40·2   1. Ich habe eine Waschmaschine.   2. Wir haben zwei Nachttische.   3. Es gibt drei Zimmer.   4. Sie haben eine Spülmaschine.   5. Es gibt zwei Sessel im Wohnzimmer.   6. Es gibt ein Telefon in der Küche.   7. Hast du einen Kühlschrank?   8. Er hat keinen Trockner.

40·3   1. Ich stelle die Lampe auf den Tisch.   2. Die Lampe steht auf dem Tisch.   3. Ich setze die Katze unter den Stuhl.   4. Die Katze sitzt unter dem Stuhl.   5. Ich lege die Zeitung auf die Couch.   6. Die Zeitung liegt auf der Couch.   7. Ich hänge das Poster an die Wand über das Bett.   8. Das Poster hängt an der Wand über dem Bett.

40·4   1. an   2. zwischen   3. vor   4. in   5. an   6. über   7. unter   8. an   9. neben   10. auf

41·1   1. Mit wem   2. Womit   3. Wovor   4. Worüber   5. Über wen   6. Worauf   7. An wen   8. Worunter

41·2   1. Ja, ich bin dagegen.   2. Ja, ich bin dafür.   3. Ja, ich denke daran.   4. Ja, sie sitzt darauf.   5. Ja, ich gehe dahin.   6. Ja, ich habe schon darüber gesprochen.   7. Ja, er liegt darunter.   8. Ja, ich stehe daneben.   9. Ja, ich stehe neben ihr.   10. Ja, ich gehe dahin.

41·3   1. Worauf sitzt er?   2. Woran hat sie das Bild gehängt?   3. Womit fliegen wir/fliegt ihr nach Istanbul?   4. Woran/An wen glaubst du?   5. Von wem hat das Mädchen das Kleid bekommen?   6. Wonach fragt der Lehrer?   7. Woraus kommen die Tiere?   8. Wozu dient das?   9. Worin sitzt die Katze?   10. Wohin fliegen wir/fliegt ihr?

42·1   1. Mein Vater kauft morgen einen Rasenmäher.   2. Unsere Mutter gießt am Nachmittag die Blumen.   3. Wir gehen nach der Schule in ein Café.   4. Meine Freunde wollen heute Abend ins Kino gehen und einen Film schauen.   5. Wir basteln am Wochenende ein Modellauto.   6. Ich soll vor dem Training nichts essen.   7. Sie sehen uns bis nächste Woche nicht.

42·2   1. Um 19 Uhr gehen wir ins Kino.   2. Im Café essen wir ein Eis.   3. Mit dem Rad fahren wir nach Hause.   4. Einen Blumenstrauß schenken wir Oma zum Geburtstag.   5. Unseren Eltern geben wir das

Geschenk.   6. Meinen Freund Axel sehen wir nach der Schule.   7. Am Sonntag kann ich am Wochenende mit dir Tennis spielen.   8. Nach Griechenland fährt die Familie Schmitt in den Ferien.

42·3   1. T   2. P   3. M   4. T   5. T   6. M   7. T   8. P   9. T   10. P

42·4   1. Spielst du Tennis?   2. Isst sie Fleisch?   3. Macht er seine Hausaufgaben?   4. Ist das eine Maus?   5. Gehen wir in die Schule?   6. Laufen sie Ski?   7. Kochen wir heute Abend?

42·5   1. Wann gehen wir in die Stadt?   2. Wer hat die Hausaufgabe nicht gemacht?   3. Wo ist das Konzert?   4. Warum können wir nicht zu Hause bleiben?   5. Wem schickst du den Brief?   6. Wann fängt der Englischkurs an?   7. Wie oft fütterst du die Katze?   8. Wer ruft uns so spät an?   9. Wo arbeitest du?   10. Was willst du heute Abend machen?

43·1   1. Ich möchte schwimmen gehen, aber es ist kalt.   2. Meine Freunde sind nett, und sie sind auch schön.   3. Er möchte nicht ins Kino gehen, sondern er will zu Hause bleiben.   4. Meine Familie isst zu Weihnachten Gans, oder wir essen Ente.   5. Wir spielen Golf, aber ihr spielt Tennis.   6. Er trinkt keine Milch, sondern er trinkt lieber Cola.   7. Wir lernen heute Abend, denn wir haben morgen einen Test.   8. Du kommst nicht mit, denn du bist krank.   9. Die Mädchen singen, oder sie spielen Gitarre.   10. Meine Mutter arbeitet, und mein Vater bleibt zu Hause.

44·1   1. Magda kann nicht ins Kino gehen, weil sie zu Hause helfen muss.   2. Als ich nur vier Jahre alt war, konnte ich schon Fahrrad fahren.   3. Wir können nicht essen, bis das Essen fertig ist.   4. Wenn ich eine Million Dollar hätte, würde ich ein großes Haus kaufen.   5. Während meine Eltern weg sind, bin ich alleine zu Hause.   6. Mein Cousin macht einen Kurs, damit er Elektriker werden kann.   7. Sie gehen ein Eis essen, nachdem sie den Film gesehen haben.   8. Wir bringen die Gartenmöbel herein, bevor es dunkel wird.   9. Sofia kauft den Mantel nicht, da sie nicht genug Geld hat.   10. Weißt du, dass die Post um die Ecke ist?

44·2   1. der   2. die   3. das   4. die   5. den   6. den   7. dem   8. deren   9. denen   10. das

44·3   1. Wo ist die Tasche, die ich gestern gekauft habe?   2. Meine Eltern kennen einen Mann, der Weltmeister in Fußball ist.   3. Siehst du die Frau, deren Mutter gestorben ist?   4. Hier ist ein Kuli, den du borgen kannst.   5. Wir haben einen Film gesehen, der stinklangweilig war.   6. Hier ist ein Mädchen, dem ich helfe.   7. Kennst du die Frau, deren Freund ihr einen Blumenstrauß gegeben hat?   8. Mein Bruder ist ein Mensch, mit dem man gut Schach spielen kann.   9. Der Fluß, der durch Frankfurt fließt, heißt die Oder.   10. Deutsch ist ein Fach, das Spaß macht.

45·1   1. nach Frankreich zu fahren.   2. einen schönen Urlaub zu machen.   3. ein Haus zu kaufen.   4. viel Geld zu verdienen.   5. in Ordnung zu sein.   6. die Hausaufgaben zu machen.   7. einen Regenschirm mitzunehmen.   8. die See zu sehen.   9. Spaß zu haben.   10. abends spät nach Hause zu kommen.

45·2   1. Statt zuzuhören, macht sie was sie will.   2. Statt langsamer zu fahren, rast sie auf der Autobahn.   3. Statt genug Geld mitzunehmen, kann sie nichts kaufen.   4. Statt mit den Eltern in Urlaub zu fahren, bleibt sie in den Ferien zu Hause.   5. Statt zu schauen, fährt sie einfach los.

46·1   1. fünf   2. drei   3. zehn   4. hundert   5. sechsundfünfzig   6. fünfundsechzig   7. neunzig   8. dreiunddreißig   9. zweiundfünfzig   10. siebenundachtzig   11. eine Million   12. tausendneunhundertneunundneunzig

46·2   1. fünfzehn Uhr   2. acht Uhr fünf   3. zwanzig Uhr fünfundfünfzig   4. zwei Uhr zweiundzwanzig   5. zehn Uhr siebzehn   6. ein Uhr achtundvierzig   7. einundzwanzig Uhr neun   8. neun Uhr einundzwanzig   9. fünf Uhr zwei   10. sechs Uhr fünfunddreißig

46·3   1. am Samstag und am Sonntag   2. am Sonntag   3. am Montag   4. am Sonntag   5. am Freitag   6. am Dienstag

46·4   1. am fünfundzwanzigsten Dezember   2. am dritten Oktober   3. am vierten Juli   4. am einunddreißigsten Oktober   5. am sechsten Januar   6. am sechsten Dezember   7. am ersten November   8. am ersten Januar   9. am vierzehnten Februar   10. am zweiundzwanzigsten oder am dreiundzwanzigsten September

46·5   1. im Dezember   2. im Juni   3. im Dezember   4. im November oder Dezember   5. im Februar   6. im August oder im September   7. im Juli und im August   8. im Januar und im Februar   9. im März, April, Mai, und Juni   10. im Mai

The original ordinal number

In 1897 Georg Cantor created the ordinal number. He was a German mathematician who was born in Russia. Ordinal numbers define the relationship between the cardinal numbers. They cannot be made into negative numbers.